MW01115824

Blackstone Outdoor Gas Griddle Cookbook for Beginners

1800 Days of Mouthwatering Recipes for Your Grilling Adventures | Easy Griddle Recipes, Tips, and Techniques for American Grilling Enthusiasts

Harigald Vhford

© **Copyright 2024 Harigald Vhford - All Rights Reserved.**

It is in no way legal to reproduce, duplicate, or transmit any part of this document by either electronic means or in printed format. Recording of this publication is strictly prohibited, and any storage of this material is not allowed unless with written permission from the publisher. All rights reserved.

The information provided herein is stated to be truthful and consistent, in that any liability, regarding inattention or otherwise, by any usage or abuse of any policies, processes, or directions contained within is the solitary and complete responsibility of the recipient reader. Under no circumstances will any legal liability or blame be held against the publisher for any reparation, damages, or monetary loss due to the information herein, either directly or indirectly.

Respective authors own all copyrights not held by the publisher.

Legal Notice:

This book is copyright protected. This is only for personal use. You cannot amend, distribute, sell, use, quote or paraphrase any part of the content within this book without the consent of the author or copyright owner. Legal action will be pursued if this is breached.

Disclaimer Notice:

Please note the information contained within this document is for educational and entertainment purposes only. Every attempt has been made to provide accurate, up-to-date, reliable, and complete information. No warranties of any kind are expressed or implied. Readers acknowledge that the author is not engaging in the rendering of legal, financial, medical or professional advice.

By reading this document, the reader agrees that under no circumstances are we responsible for any losses, direct or indirect, which are incurred as a result of the use of information contained within this document, including, but not limited to, errors, omissions, or inaccuracies.

Table of Contents

INTRODUCTION

Which Blackstone Is Right for You?

Choosing the right Blackstone griddle depends on several factors, including your cooking needs, available space, and budget. Blackstone offers various models that cater to different preferences and requirements:

Size and Cooking Area: Blackstone griddles come in several sizes, typically measured by the cooking surface in square inches. The smaller models, like the 17-inch or 22-inch, are portable and ideal for smaller groups or limited outdoor spaces such as balconies or patios. They are easier to transport and store but offer less cooking space compared to larger models.

For larger gatherings or more extensive cooking needs, the 28-inch, 36-inch, or even 48-inch models provide ample cooking area. These larger sizes are suitable for cooking multiple items simultaneously, making them perfect for hosting backyard parties or family gatherings where you want to prepare a variety of foods at once.

Portability: If you plan to use your griddle in different locations or for camping trips, portability is a crucial factor. Smaller models are easier to transport due to their size and weight, whereas larger models with foldable legs or wheels offer more convenience if you need to move the griddle around your yard or take it on the go.

Accessories and Features: Consider what additional features are important to you. Some Blackstone griddles come with side shelves for extra workspace or hooks to hang utensils. Others have built-in storage cabinets or even warming drawers. These features can enhance your cooking experience and organization, but they also affect the overall footprint and setup of the griddle.

Fuel Type: Most Blackstone griddles are powered by propane, but there are also models that use natural gas. The choice between these typically depends on your preference and access to the respective fuel source. Propane models offer flexibility in terms of where you can use the griddle, while natural gas models provide convenience if you have a gas line installed in your outdoor cooking area.

Budget: Finally, your budget will play a significant role in determining which Blackstone griddle is right for you. Smaller models are generally more affordable, while larger and more feature-rich models can be pricier. Consider how often you'll use the griddle and what features are essential versus nice-to-have to make the most cost-effective decision.

In conclusion, when choosing a Blackstone griddle, assess your cooking needs, available space, portability requirements, desired features, fuel preferences, and budget. This evaluation will help you select the model that best fits your lifestyle and ensures enjoyable outdoor cooking experiences.

How To Start Cooking on Your Blackstone Griddle?

Cooking on a Blackstone griddle can be a delightful experience, offering versatility and the ability to cook various foods simultaneously. Here's a comprehensive guide on how to get started with your Blackstone griddle:

- Preparation:

  easoning the Griddle: Before your first use, it's crucial to season the griddle to create a non-stick surface and prevent rusting. Coat the griddle top with a high smoke point oil (e.g., vegetable oil, flaxseed oil) and heat it until it starts smoking. Let it cool and repeat the process several times.

  leaning: Ensure the griddle surface is clean before heating. Use a griddle scraper to remove any debris or leftover seasoning from previous uses. Wipe it down with a damp cloth or paper towel.

- Starting the Griddle:

  ropane Setup: If your griddle is propane-powered, ensure the propane tank is connected and turned on. Open the griddle's gas valve and ignite the burners using the ignition system. Adjust the heat settings to your desired temperature.

  reheating: Allow the griddle to preheat for 10-15 minutes. This ensures even cooking and prevents food from sticking.

- Cooking:

  il the Surface: Before cooking, lightly oil the griddle surface to prevent sticking. Use a brush or a paper towel to spread a thin layer of oil.

emperature Control: Blackstone griddles typically have adjustable heat zones. Use higher heat for searing meats and lower heat for more delicate foods or to keep items warm.

- Cooking Techniques:

earing: For steaks, burgers, or vegetables, use high heat to achieve a caramelized exterior while keeping the inside juicy.

tir-frying: Push ingredients around quickly with a spatula to cook them evenly and achieve a slight char.

mash Burgers: Press balls of ground beef onto the griddle with a spatula for crispy edges.

ggs and Pancakes: Use lower heat and a small amount of oil to prevent sticking.

anaging Grease: Blackstone griddles have built-in grease management systems. Empty the grease cup regularly to prevent flare-ups and maintain cleanliness.

- Cleaning and Maintenance:

  fter Cooking: Once done, scrape any food residue into the grease cup using a griddle scraper. Wipe down the griddle with a damp cloth or paper towel.

  easoning After Use: After cleaning, apply a thin layer of oil to the griddle surface while it's warm to maintain its non-stick properties and prevent rust.

- Storage:

  ool Down: Allow the griddle to cool completely before covering or storing it.

  overing: Use a griddle cover to protect it from the elements and keep it clean between uses.

By following these steps, you'll be able to start cooking effectively on your Blackstone griddle and explore its full potential for preparing delicious meals outdoors. With practice, you'll discover new techniques and recipes that showcase the versatility and enjoyment of griddle cooking.

Proper Seasoning with Blackstone Griddle

Proper seasoning of your Blackstone Griddle is crucial for both maintaining its longevity and enhancing the flavor of your food. Seasoning refers to the process of creating a non-stick surface on the griddle by building up layers of oil that polymerize to form a durable coating. This process not only prevents rust but also helps in achieving that coveted restaurant-quality sear and flavor in your cooking. Here's a detailed guide on how to properly season your Blackstone Griddle:

Why Seasoning is Important

Prevents Rust: The primary purpose of seasoning is to create a protective layer that prevents the griddle from rusting. The metal of the griddle is exposed to air and moisture, which can lead to oxidation and rust formation over time if not properly protected.

Non-Stick Surface: Seasoning creates a natural non-stick surface on the griddle. This is essential for cooking delicate foods like eggs, pancakes, and fish, which can easily stick to an unseasoned surface.

Enhances Flavor: A well-seasoned griddle imparts a unique flavor to your food. The oils used in seasoning can enhance the taste and texture of your dishes, providing a subtle richness that is difficult to achieve with other cooking methods.

How to Season Your Blackstone Griddle

Initial Cleaning: Before seasoning your griddle for the first time, it's crucial to

clean it thoroughly. Remove any protective coatings or residues left from the manufacturing process using warm, soapy water and a sponge. Rinse the griddle thoroughly and dry it completely with a towel.

Applying Oil: Once dry, apply a thin layer of high-heat cooking oil (such as vegetable oil, flaxseed oil, or canola oil) to the entire surface of the griddle, including the sides and corners. Use a paper towel or cloth to spread the oil evenly and ensure there are no pools or excess oil.

Heating the Griddle: Turn on your Blackstone Griddle to medium-high heat. Allow the griddle to heat up until it starts smoking. Heating the griddle helps the oil to penetrate the metal pores and create the non-stick surface.

Cooling Down and Repeating: Once the griddle starts smoking, let it cool down naturally. After it has cooled completely, repeat the oil application and heating process at least two more times. Each cycle helps to build up the seasoning layer, making it more effective and durable.

Regular Maintenance: After the initial seasoning, maintain the griddle by cleaning it after each use. Use a scraper or spatula to remove food debris while the griddle is still warm (not hot). Avoid using soap as it can break down the seasoning layer. Instead, wipe the griddle with a damp cloth or paper towel and reapply a thin layer of oil if necessary.

Storage: Store your Blackstone Griddle in a dry place to prevent rust. If storing for an extended period, apply a light coat of oil to the griddle surface to maintain the seasoning.

Tips for Success

Use the Right Oil: Choose oils with a high smoke point for seasoning, as they will withstand the high temperatures needed to polymerize on the griddle surface.

Even Application: Ensure the oil is spread evenly across the griddle to prevent uneven seasoning or sticky spots.

Patience is Key: Seasoning a griddle takes time and multiple layers of oil. Don't rush the process; each layer adds to the griddle's performance and durability.

Consistency: Regularly maintain and re-season your griddle to keep it in optimal condition. The more you use and care for it, the better it will perform.

By following these steps and tips, you can effectively season your Blackstone Griddle to create a non-stick surface that enhances the flavor of your food and ensures the longevity of your cooking equipment. Proper seasoning not only improves the cooking experience but also allows you to enjoy the full potential of your outdoor gas griddle for years to come.

The Difference Between Blackstone and Other Grills

The Blackstone Outdoor Gas Griddle stands out distinctly from traditional grills in several key aspects, making it a versatile and appealing choice for outdoor cooking enthusiasts. Understanding the differences between the Blackstone Griddle and other types of grills helps highlight its unique features and benefits.

Cooking Surface

One of the most significant differences between the Blackstone Griddle and traditional grills is the cooking surface itself. While traditional grills typically

feature a grid of metal bars or grates where food is placed, the Blackstone Griddle boasts a smooth, flat cooking surface made of cold-rolled steel or non-stick coated steel. This surface is similar to what you'd find in restaurant kitchens on a flat-top grill, providing several advantages:

Versatility: The smooth surface of the Blackstone Griddle allows for cooking a wide variety of foods that might not be as easily manageable on a traditional grill. This includes items like pancakes, eggs, stir-fries, and even delicate items like fish or thinly sliced vegetables.

Even Cooking: Unlike grills where food can fall through the gaps or get uneven heat distribution, the Blackstone Griddle ensures even heat across the entire cooking surface. This consistency is crucial for achieving perfectly cooked food without hot spots.

Increased Cooking Area: Griddles often have a larger cooking surface area compared to traditional grills of similar size, allowing you to cook more food at once. This is advantageous when preparing meals for larger groups or when cooking multiple dishes simultaneously.

Cooking Techniques

The cooking techniques used on a Blackstone Griddle differ from those employed on traditional grills, primarily due to the nature of the cooking surface:

Direct vs. Indirect Heat: Traditional grills rely heavily on direct heat from below (via gas burners or charcoal) and indirect heat (from the sides or top) to cook food. In contrast, the Blackstone Griddle primarily uses direct heat applied uniformly across the entire surface. This makes it easier to control cooking temperatures and speeds up the cooking process for many dishes.

Temperature Control: Griddles typically offer more precise temperature control than traditional grills. This allows for precise adjustments when cooking different

types of food, from searing meats at high temperatures to gently cooking delicate items at lower heats.

Cleaning and Maintenance

Maintaining and cleaning a Blackstone Griddle differs significantly from caring for a traditional grill:

Seasoning: Griddles often require seasoning similar to cast iron cookware. This involves applying a thin layer of oil and heating it to create a natural non-stick surface. Seasoning helps prevent food from sticking and protects the steel from rust.

Cleaning: Cleaning a Blackstone Griddle is typically easier than cleaning a traditional grill grate. The flat surface allows for straightforward scraping and wiping down after cooking. Some models even feature built-in grease management systems to channel grease away from the cooking surface.

Outdoor Cooking Experience

The Blackstone Griddle offers a unique outdoor cooking experience that differs from traditional grills:

Social Cooking: The large, flat cooking surface encourages communal cooking experiences, where multiple people can cook together simultaneously. This makes it ideal for backyard gatherings and family events.

Adaptability: The versatility of the Blackstone Griddle extends beyond typical grilling to encompass a wide range of cooking styles, from breakfast to dinner and everything in between. This adaptability appeals to users looking to expand their outdoor cooking repertoire.

In summary, while traditional grills have their advantages in terms of smoky flavor and char marks, the Blackstone Outdoor Gas Griddle stands out with its versatile cooking surface, precise temperature control, ease of cleaning, and ability to cook a wide variety of foods. Whether you're a beginner or a seasoned outdoor chef, the Blackstone Griddle offers a unique and enjoyable cooking experience that can elevate your outdoor culinary adventures.

Tips, And Techniques for Grilling Enthusiasts

Griddling on a Blackstone outdoor gas griddle offers a unique cooking experience that combines the best of grilling and griddling techniques. Whether you're a beginner or an experienced griller, mastering tips and techniques can elevate your outdoor cooking game significantly.

- Temperature Control:

   ontrolling the temperature is key to achieving perfect results. Blackstone griddles often have multiple burners, allowing you to create different temperature zones. Preheat the griddle thoroughly before cooking, and adjust the heat according to what you're cooking—higher heat for searing and lower heat for more delicate items.

- Using Different Cooking Zones:

   tilize the different heat zones on your griddle to your advantage. One side can be kept hotter for searing meats or creating a char, while the other side can be cooler for keeping food warm or cooking more delicate items like vegetables.

Techniques for Griddling Success

- Searing vs. Cooking Through:

   or meats, searing at high heat initially locks in juices and flavor. Once seared, you

can move the meat to a cooler zone to finish cooking through without burning the exterior. This technique is particularly effective for steaks, burgers, and chops.

- Managing Flare-Ups:

  riddles can generate flare-ups from grease or oil drippings. Be prepared to move food away from flare-ups or have a spray bottle with water handy to control flames without affecting the cooking temperature.

- Perfecting Breakfast Favorites:

  riddles excel at cooking breakfast items like pancakes, eggs, bacon, and hash browns. Use a little oil or butter to prevent sticking, and adjust the heat as needed to ensure even cooking without burning.

- Stir-Frying and Sauteing:

  he large, flat surface of a griddle is perfect for stir-frying vegetables, seafood, or thinly sliced meats. Keep ingredients moving to ensure even cooking, and use sauces or seasonings that complement the charred flavors imparted by the griddle.

- Keeping It Clean:

  fter cooking, while the griddle is still warm, scrape off any food residues with a metal spatula designed for griddle cleaning. Once cooled, wipe down with a damp cloth and mild soap if necessary. Regular maintenance ensures your griddle stays in top condition.

Tips for Enhancing Flavor

- Marinades and Seasonings:

se marinades and dry rubs to add depth of flavor to meats and vegetables before cooking. The griddle's intense heat caramelizes sugars and spices, enhancing the taste of your dishes.

- Experimenting with Ingredients:

riddling opens up possibilities for creative cooking. Try griddling fruits like pineapple or peaches for a caramelized dessert, or griddle halloumi cheese for a unique appetizer.

- Adding Smoky Flavor:

hile griddles don't impart smoke like traditional grills, you can achieve a hint of smokiness by using wood chips in a smoker box or pouch placed on the griddle while cooking. This method works well for meats and vegetables alike.

- Finishing Touches:

ust before serving, consider adding a finishing touch like a drizzle of balsamic reduction, a sprinkle of fresh herbs, or a dollop of compound butter to elevate flavors and presentation.

Advanced Techniques to Explore

- Reverse Searing:

tart by cooking thicker cuts of meat on a lower heat to cook them evenly. Finish by searing on a hot part of the griddle for a perfectly cooked steak or roast.

- Griddling Seafood:

rom shrimp and scallops to fish fillets, seafood cooks quickly on a griddle. Ensure the surface is well-oiled and cook until just opaque to retain moisture and flavor.

- Griddle Baking:

es, you can bake on a griddle! Use a cast iron skillet or griddle-friendly baking dish to make biscuits, cornbread, or even pizza right on the griddle surface.

By mastering these tips and techniques, you'll unlock the full potential of your Blackstone outdoor gas griddle. Experiment with different recipes and ingredients to discover your favorite griddling styles and flavors. Whether you're cooking for breakfast, lunch, dinner, or dessert, the griddle's versatility ensures there's always something new and delicious to create. Happy griddling!

Chapter 1: Breakfast

Chopped Italian Sandwich

Prep Time: 15 minutes   Cook Time: 20 minutes   Serves: 6

Ingredients:

Sandwiches
- 3 Italian sub bread loaves
- 3/4 cup mayonnaise
- 10 slices sandwich-sized pepperoni
- 10 slices sandwich-sized salami
- 10 slices ham
- 10 slices provolone cheese
- 3 cups shredded romaine lettuce
- 3 tablespoons diced pickled yellow peppers

Dressing
- 3 tablespoons red wine vinegar
- 2 tablespoons olive oil
- 1 tablespoon Italian seasoning blend
- 1/2 teaspoon salt

Directions:

1. Preheat your griddle over medium heat. Let it heat up for 10 minutes, minimum.
2. While the griddle is preheating, slice the bread loaves in half, leaving them connected on one side.
3. Spread the mayo evenly on both sides of each loaf of bread.
4. Take the meat and cut it into 1/2" cubes.
5. Mix up all of the dressing ingredients and whisk briskly until it is emulsified.
6. Put the chopped meat down on the griddle along with the cut bread loaves, mayo-side down.
7. Flip the meat over a few times until it is hot and sizzling and some of it is getting some browned bits on the edges.
8. Cook the bread, pressing down gently on the top as needed, until it is golden brown and toasty.
9. Pull the bread off the griddle and immediately place 3 cheese slices on each loaf.
10. Carefully remove the cooked meat from the griddle and put it on the bread loaves.
11. Toss the lettuce with the dressing and load that up on the subs too. Close, cut in half, and enjoy!

Nutritional Value (Amount per Serving):

Calories: 581; Fat: 35.91; Carb: 37.48; Protein: 27.21

Blackstone Steak and Egg Bagel Sandwich

Prep Time: 5 minutes   Cook Time: 10 minutes   Serves: 4

Ingredients:

- 1 pound steak (sirloin, New York, and Ribeye work well!)
- 1 teaspoon salt
- ½ teaspoon black pepper
- 1 tablespoon Worcestershire sauce
- 2 tablespoons of butter, divided
- 4 eggs
- 4 slices of cheddar cheese
- 4 everything bagels

Directions:

1. Preheat your Blackstone to medium-high for 10-15 minutes before starting.
2. Cut the steak into ½ inch strips.
3. Season the steak with salt and pepper.
4. Put 1 tablespoon of butter on your Blackstone. Let it melt, and add the steak in a single layer on top. Cook for 1 minute, flip, and cook an additional 1 minute. (A little more if you like your steak medium-well to well instead of medium-rare to medium.)
5. Remove the steak and set aside, covered.
6. Next, add the remaining tablespoon of butter to the griddle. Crack your eggs over the butter. Flip once after the white is mostly set, or dome immediately if you want to skip the flip. Cook until the white is set, and the yolk is your desired texture.
7. Toast the cut side of the bagels on the griddle surface.
8. Place the steak on the bottom of the bagels, then add the egg and place the cheese on top.
9. Eat immediately or wrap in foil and then place in a ziplock bag for meal prep.

Nutritional Value (Amount per Serving):

Calories: 670; Fat: 29.49; Carb: 50.82; Protein: 69.96

Blackstone Salmon Sandwich

Prep Time: 10 minutes   Cook Time: 15 minutes   Serves: 4

Ingredients:

Salmon Sandwiches
- 4 salmon filets, sandwich-sized
- 1 tablespoon olive oil

- Midnight Toker Rub
- 1 teaspoon salt

Dill Aioli
- 1/2 cup mayonnaise
- 1/2 teaspoon lemon zest
- 2 teaspoons lemon juice

- 4 toasted buns
- baby arugula

- 1/4 teaspoon salt
- 1/2 teaspoon minced fresh dill

Directions:

1. Mix together all of the dill mayo ingredients and place them into the fridge. Preheat your Blackstone griddle to medium heat.
2. Brush each salmon filet with olive oil, and then dust liberally with Midnight Toker and salt.
3. Place the fillets on the griddle and cook until the internal temperature reaches 130°-135°F, or until it reaches the temp that you prefer. Toast the buns.
4. Remove the filets from the griddle and let sit for 5 minutes.
5. Spread some of the aioli on the toasted buns, top with salmon filet, lettuce, and the other bun, and serve hot!

Nutritional Value (Amount per Serving):

Calories: 813; Fat: 43.28; Carb: 34.56; Protein: 71.62

Blackened Fish Sandwich

Prep Time: 10 minutes   Cook Time: 10 minutes   Serves: 6

Ingredients:

- 6 white fish filets, skinless
- 2 tablespoons blackening seasoning
- 2 tablespoons olive oil

- 6 brioche buns
- baby arugula
- tartar sauce or mayo

Directions:

1. Season the filets with the blackening seasoning on both sides and set aside.
2. Preheat your Blackstone over medium-low heat for 10-15 minutes.
3. Put down a thin coat of oil and place the fish down on the griddle. Cook for 4-5 minutes per side.
4. Remove from the griddle and set aside.
5. Toast the buns and top with the fish and some baby arugula and tartar sauce or mayo, if so desired.

Nutritional Value (Amount per Serving):

Calories: 637; Fat: 39.63; Carb: 50.97; Protein: 17.67

Blackstone Monte Cristo

Prep Time: 15 minutes   Cook Time: 10 minutes   Serves: 6

Ingredients:

- 4 eggs
- 1/3 cup half and half
- 12 pieces of white bread
- 2 tablespoons mayo
- 2 tablespoons mustard
- 18 thin slices swiss or gruyere cheese
- 2 pounds deli thin-sliced ham
- powdered sugar
- raspberry jam

Directions:

1. Preheat your griddle over medium-low heat.
2. Take the eggs and half and half and whip them together until combined in a large shallow dish.
3. Drench ONE side of your bread in the egg wash. Set down on a parchment-lined baking sheet, eggy side down, in a single layer.
4. Spread 1 teaspoon of mayo and 1 teaspoon of mustard on each sandwich bread pair, with mayo on one piece and mustard on the other.
5. Place one piece of cheese on each slice of bread. Evenly distribute the ham across all 12 pieces of bread.
6. Take the remaining 6 slices of cheese and place it on ONE half of each sandwich bread pair. (You want there to be 3 pieces of cheese in each sandwich.)
7. Marry the sandwich halves to make full sandwiches.
8. Generously butter the griddle and place the sandwiches onto it. Press down gently with a large spatula, and cover.
9. Cook until the bread is browned and the egg mixture is set, and then flip it over and cook covered on the other side until browned.
10. Remove and dust with powdered sugar and serve with a side of raspberry jam.

Nutritional Value (Amount per Serving):

Calories: 998; Fat: 58.32; Carb: 70.07; Protein: 46.39

Blackstone Griddle Eggs in a Basket

Prep Time: 5 minutes   Cook Time: 10 minutes   Serves: 6

Ingredients:

- 6 slices bread
- 6 tablespoons butter
- 6 fresh eggs
- salt and pepper
- canola oil, for the griddle

Directions:

1. Preheat your Blackstone griddle over medium-low heat.
2. While the griddle is heating up, butter BOTH sides of your bread and cut out the middle of each piece with a serrated knife, gently. Safe these pieces, you'll be toasting them on the griddle!
3. Bring your eggs and bread out and place the bread on the griddle. Let the first side toast, and then flip the bread over. Toast the cut-out pieces on both sides.
4. Crack an egg into each of the holes, sprinkle with salt and pepper, and cover all with a large lid or melting dome(s).
5. Cook until the whites are set but the yolks are still runny. Only flip if you are really brave, chances of yolk breakage are high.

Nutritional Value (Amount per Serving):

Calories: 330; Fat: 26.58; Carb: 11.65; Protein: 10.97

Blackstone Runza

Prep Time: 5 minutes   Cook Time: 20 minutes   Serves: 6

Ingredients:

- 2 tablespoons butter
- 6 cups shredded cabbage
- 1 large onion, sliced
- 1/2 teaspoon seasoning salt (like Lawry's or Johnny's)
- 1 pound ground beef (80/20 blend)
- 1/2 teaspoon salt
- 1/2 teaspoon pepper
- 1/2 teaspoon garlic powder
- 1/2 teaspoon onion powder
- 6 slices American cheese (or cheddar if you aren't into American)
- 1 tube crescent roll dough sheet

Directions:

1. Preheat your Blackstone over medium heat.
2. On half of the griddle, put down some butter and cook the onions.
3. Remove from the griddle ones they are soft and lightly browned.
4. On the other half, put down some more butter and cook the cabbage.

5. Remove to the onion plate when it is softened and cooked.
6. Season the ground beef and cook on the Blackstone until it is browned.
7. Take the crescent roll sheet out of the fridge, and place it onto the griddle.
8. Spread the filling over half of it, leaving room on the sides open.
9. Cover with cheese and fold over the other half of the dough sheet.
10. Flip once if you have the skills. Cover the Runza and turn the heat off if you don't.
11. Cut into pieces and serve. (With a fork. This isn't a hand-held sandwich in this form.)

Nutritional Value (Amount per Serving):

Calories: 400; Fat: 25.98; Carb: 13.49; Protein: 28.24

Blackstone Philly Cheesesteak

Prep Time: 5 minutes   Cook Time: 10 minutes   Serves: 6

Ingredients:

- 3 pounds thinly sliced ribeye
- 1 tablespoon oil
- salt
- pepper
- provolone or cheese whiz
- buns
- butter
- peppers and onions (optional)

Directions:

1. Preheat your gas griddle over medium heat until it is preheated. Butter your buns and give them a quick toast.
2. On one half of the griddle, put down some butter and the onions and peppers if you are going that direction, and on the other half throw down some oil. Let it preheat, but not quite smoking, and then put the beef on.
3. Salt and pepper the beef according to your preferences, and more around continuously with large metal spatulas,
4. Top with cheese, cover with a dome and turn OFF the griddle. The residual heat will melt the cheese.
5. Load up your buns with cheese-covered ribeye, top with any peppers and onions that you want, and chow!

Nutritional Value (Amount per Serving):

Calories: 817; Fat: 70.28; Carb: 6.97; Protein: 39.57

Blackstone Steak Quesadilla

Prep Time: 5 minutes   Cook Time: 10 minutes   Serves: 6

Ingredients:

- 12 flour tortillas
- 3 cups cooked steak (approximately. You can use more or less if you'd like!)
- 1 tablespoon chili lime seasoning (or your favorite)
- 3 cups shredded Mexican-blend cheese
- oil for greasing the griddle

Directions:

1. Fire up the griddle over medium to medium-high heat.
2. Lay down a little oil and then place the leftover steak onto the griddle and sprinkle with the chili lime seasoning.
3. Cook for 1-2 minutes, just long enough to heat it up.
4. Place a little more oil down, and put a tortilla on top followed by cheese, meat, more cheese, and another tortilla.
5. Cover the quesadilla with a melting lid and cook for 2-3 minutes.
6. Flip, and cook on the other side for an additional 2-3 minutes, and then repeat until all of the quesadillas are cooked.

Nutritional Value (Amount per Serving):

Calories: 618; Fat: 29.03; Carb: 49.3; Protein: 39.29

Blackstone Sausage-Stuffed Hash Browns

Prep Time: 20 minutes   Cook Time: 30 minutes   Serves: 6

Ingredients:

- 3 cups dehydrated hash browns
- 3 cups hot water
- 1/4 cup finely diced onions
- 1/4 cup butter
- 10 pieces thick-sliced bacon
- 1/2 pound breakfast sausage
- 1/4 - 1/3 cup oil
- Salt, pepper, and garlic
- 2 cups shredded cheddar cheese

Directions:

1. Place your hash browns and the hot water in a bowl, and let soak for about 15 minutes. Drain the excess water.
2. While the hash browns are soaking, preheat your gas griddle over medium-high heat. Cook the bacon and the breakfast sausage, and set aside when finished.
3. Place about a tablespoon of butter down, and cook the onions for 3-4 minutes.
4. Place the hash browns on the griddle, and put a tablespoon or two of oil down by drizzling it over the hash browns.
5. Cook for several minutes, or until the bottom has developed a golden-

brown crust. Flip with a large spatula, and drizzle with some more oil. Place cheese and sausage over half of the hash browns.

6. Once the bottom side is browned, flip the half that is not topped with sausage and cheese over the top, sandwiching in the sausage and egg.
7. Top with bacon slices and additional cheese, turn the griddle down to low heat, and cover. Cook until the cheese is melted.

Nutritional Value (Amount per Serving):

Calories: 729; Fat: 57.5; Carb: 31.63; Protein: 23.63

Hash Brown Omelette

Prep Time: 15 minutes   Cook Time: 20 minutes   Serves: 6

Ingredients:

- 30 ounces shredded hash browns thawed
- 4 Tablespoons butter
- 12 large eggs
- 1/4 cup milk
- 2 cups grated cheddar cheese
- 1 cup diced ham
- 1/4 cup finely diced onion
- 1 Tablespoon Gimme Some Grilling Sweet and Smoky Rub

Directions:

1. Preheat the Blackstone griddle over medium heat. Brush the grill with 4 Tablespoons of butter.
2. In a small bowl combine eggs and milk, whisk until well incorporated. Set aside.
3. Spread the hash browns out on the griddle and toss with melted butter. Then spread them into a rectangle, making sure they are in an even thin layer, on one half of the griddle. Sprinkle with Sweet & Smoky Rub. Allow the hash browns to cook until lightly golden brown, about 10 minutes.
4. On the other side of the griddle place the chopped ham and onions turning frequently until onions are translucent.
5. When the hash browns are golden brown on the bottom pour the egg mixture over the top. Spread evenly with the back of a spatula.
6. Then sprinkle 1 1/2 cups grated cheese over the egg mixture.
7. Top with ham and onions, cook eggs 3-5 minutes or until eggs are set.
8. Using a large long mutual spatula, cut the rectangle of hash browns in half width wise and in half lengthwise. Slide the metal spatula underneath the hash browns to loosen them from the griddle, then fold one end of the omelets toward the other hand, folding it in half. Repeat with remaining

omelets.

9. Top each omelet with remaining 1/2 cup of cheese. Turn off heat on the griddle. Once the cheese is slightly melted, remove from the griddle and serve with decided toppings.

Nutritional Value (Amount per Serving):

Calories: 668; Fat: 41.47; Carb: 51.09; Protein: 26.14

Bacon and Egg Breakfast Wrap

Prep Time: 10 minutes   Cook Time: 20 minutes   Serves: 3

Ingredients:

- 6 slices bacon
- 1 batch Perfect Scrambled Eggs
- 3 large flour tortillas
- 1 tablespoon canola oil

Directions:

1. Cook the bacon on the stovetop, or on your grill. Drain the excess grease and set aside.
2. Cook your fluffy scrambled eggs, melt the cheese on top and set aside.
3. Warm your tortillas for about 30 seconds in the microwave to soften them up, and then gently place some eggs and bacon inside.
4. Wrap up the eggs and bacon and fold in the ends.
5. Lightly brush a non-stick pan or your griddle with cooking oil. Preheat to medium heat and place the wrap seam-side-down in the pan.
6. Lightly press down the wrap, cook for 1-2 minutes or until it is lightly browned, and flip.
7. Cook the other side until it is also golden brown, and then eat.

Nutritional Value (Amount per Serving):

Calories: 417; Fat: 29.54; Carb: 24.85; Protein: 12.51

Chapter 2: Lunch & Dinner

Blackstone Naan

Prep Time: 1 hour 30 minutes   Cook Time: 20 minutes   Serves: 24

Ingredients:

- 2 cups warm water
- 3 tablespoons + 2 teaspoons yeast
- 2 tablespoons sugar
- 1/3 cup olive oil
- 1 cup sour cream
- 4 eggs
- 1 tablespoon salt
- 10-12 cups all-purpose flour
- 1/2 cup butter, melted
- 1 tablespoon crushed garlic
- 2 teaspoons parsley

Directions:

1. Combine the warm water, yeast, sugar, olive oil, sour cream, eggs, and salt in a bowl. Whisk to combine.
2. Add in 6 cups of the flour and stir briskly with a wooden spoon until all of the flour is absorbed into the mixture.
3. Continue adding flour, 1 cup at a time, until a soft dough forms.
4. Turn the ball of dough out onto a well-floured surface and knead for 5-6 minutes, continuing to add small amounts of flour as necessary to prevent the dough from sticking to your hands and the counter.
5. Put the kneaded dough ball into a lightly greased bowl and covered with a lightly greased piece of plastic wrap. Let rise for about an hour, or until doubled in size.
6. Dump the risen dough ball out onto a floured counter and cut into 24 equally-sized dough balls.
7. Melt the butter and mix in the garlic and parsley.
8. Preheat your griddle over medium-high heat.
9. Roll each dough ball out with a rolling pin until it is about 4-6" in diameter. You'll want to work in batches of 6-12. If you roll them ALL out and stack them all, the bottom WILL stick together before they are done cooking. Ask me how I know.
10. Keep in mind, the thicker you leave the dough the more it'll puff up.
11. Cook the dough in batches of 6 on your lightly oiled griddle. Flip after the first side gets browned and there are bubbles formed on the top. Flip, and cook until the other side is getting browned on the parts that are touching the griddle surface.
12. Flip again, brush with garlic butter, and remove from the griddle.
13. Enjoy warm!

Nutritional Value (Amount per Serving):

Calories: 308; Fat: 10; Carb: 45.51; Protein: 7.99

Smoked Pulled Pork Fried Rice

Prep Time: 5 minutes   Cook Time: 15 minutes   Serves: 8

Ingredients:

- 2 tablespoons canola oil, divided
- 1 teaspoon sesame oil
- 2 cups of mixed peas and carrots
- 1/4 cup finely diced onion
- 2 cups leftover smoked pulled pork
- 6 cups cold jasmine rice
- 4 tablespoons soy sauce
- 2 large eggs
- 1 teaspoon MSG (optional)

Directions:

1. Preheat your gas griddle over high heat. Let it get really hot. 10-15 minutes is usually necessary to ensure it is fully preheated.
2. Put 1 tablespoon of oil and a few shakes of sesame oil on the griddle. Stir fry peas, carrots, onion, and pulled pork until hot. Move to the side of the griddle to keep warm. If you can, reduce the temperature on that side of the griddle to medium-low.
3. Put another tablespoon of oil down and several more shakes of sesame oil. Stir fry cold rice over high heat for 3-4 minutes. Stir in pork and vegetables.
4. Add soy sauce to taste and stir well. Scoot rice over to one side of griddle and quickly cook the scrambled eggs. Gently mix eggs into rice mixture.
5. Sprinkle the whole thing with MSG and stir, if you are using it.
6. Serve hot.

Nutritional Value (Amount per Serving):

Calories: 477; Fat: 28; Carb: 62.01; Protein: 22.5

Beef Fried Rice

Prep Time: 5 minutes   Cook Time: 15 minutes   Serves: 6

Ingredients:

- 2 tablespoons canola oil, divided
- 1 teaspoon sesame oil
- 2 cups of mixed peas and carrots
- 1/4 cup finely diced onion
- 2 cups cubed steak
- 6 cups cold jasmine rice
- 4 tablespoons soy sauce
- 2 large eggs
- 1 teaspoon MSG (optional)

Directions:

1. Preheat your gas griddle over high heat. Let it really get hot. 10-15 minutes is usually necessary to ensure it is fully preheated.
2. Put 1 tablespoon of oil and a few shakes of sesame oil on the griddle. Stir

fry peas, carrots, onion, and steak until hot and the steak is browned on both sides. Move to the side of the griddle to keep warm. If you can, reduce the temperature on that side of the griddle to medium.

3. Put another tablespoon of oil down and several more shakes of sesame oil. Stir fry cold rice over high heat for 3-4 minutes. Stir in beef and vegetables.
4. Add soy sauce to taste and stir well. Scoot rice over to one side of griddle and quickly cook the scrambled eggs. Gently mix eggs into rice mixture.
5. Sprinkle the whole thing with MSG and stir, if you are using it.
6. Serve hot.

Nutritional Value (Amount per Serving):

Calories: 587; Fat: 38.2; Carb: 67.13; Protein: 31.48

Blackstone Kielbasa and Pierogies

Prep Time: 10 minutes   Cook Time: 25 minutes   Serves: 8

Ingredients:

- 1/2 pound thick-cut bacon
- 1/2 head cabbage, chopped
- 1 medium yellow onion, chopped
- 1 kielbasa sausages
- 1/4 cup butter
- 1 pound cheese and potato pierogies
- 1/2 teaspoon salt
- 1/2 teaspoon pepper
- 2 tablespoons apple cider vinegar
- 1 tablespoon olive oil
- 1 tablespoon stone ground mustard

Directions:

1. If your pierogies are frozen, let them thaw in the fridge.
2. Once they are thawed, preheat your griddle over medium-high heat.
3. Chop up the bacon into bite-sized pieces and cook it along with the onion and cabbage on the griddle. Remove once the bacon is crispy and the onion is caramelized. Remove from the griddle and cover to keep hot. If you have a large griddle, you can move to one side and reduce the heat to low and cover with a large dome to keep warm.
4. Slice the sausage into rounds and brown on both sides. Move over to the warm pile with the cabbage, onions, and bacon.
5. Melt the butter on the griddle and cook the pierogies until they are browned on both sides.
6. Toss everything together.
7. Whisk together the vinegar, olive oil, and mustard. Drizzle over the whole pile and toss to evenly distribute.
8. Enjoy hot with a side of sour cream (if desired.)

Nutritional Value (Amount per Serving):

Calories: 185; Fat: 12.21; Carb: 15.97; Protein: 4.84

Blackstone Mexican Pizzas

Prep Time: 10 minutes   Cook Time: 30 minutes   Serves: 6

Ingredients:

- 3 tablespoons avocado oil
- 12 small corn tortillas
- 3 cups shredded Mexican blend cheese
- 3 cups taco meat
- 1 1/2 cups seasoned pinto beans
- 1 cup diced tomato
- 1 avocado, diced
- 6 tablespoons sour cream
- 2 tablespoons hot sauce
- 3 tablespoons cilantro lime crema

Directions:

1. Preheat your Blackstone over medium heat.
2. Prep all of your ingredients ahead of time and put them on a large baking sheet. Don't forget your utensils!
3. Lay down a thin layer of oil on the griddle. Place 6 tortillas down, and quickly top with some meat, beans, and cheese.
4. Place another tortilla on top, and drizzle a little oil on the top tortilla too.
5. Let the bottom tortilla brown and crisp up, and then flip.
6. Put some more cheese on the top, now crisp tortilla. Cover all of them with a large dome (or shut the lid of your Blackstone if it came with one.)
7. Let the bottom tortilla crisp and the cheese on the top tortilla melt, and then remove from the griddle.
8. Top with the tomato, avocado, sour cream, hot sauce, and cilantro lime crema, plus any of your other favorite taco fixings.

Nutritional Value (Amount per Serving):

Calories: 719; Fat: 36.64; Carb: 68.21; Protein: 32.21

Blackstone Chicken Fried Rice

Prep Time: 5 minutes   Cook Time: 15 minutes   Serves: 6

Ingredients:

- 2 tablespoons canola oil, divided
- 1 teaspoon sesame oil
- 2 cups of mixed peas and carrots
- 1/4 cup finely diced onion
- 2 cups cubed chicken breast or thigh
- 6 cups cold jasmine rice
- 4 tablespoons soy sauce

- 2 large eggs
- 1 teaspoon MSG (optional)

Directions:

1. Preheat your gas griddle over high heat. Let it really get hot. 10-15 minutes is usually necessary to make sure it is fully preheated.
2. Put 1 tablespoon of oil and a few shakes of sesame oil on the griddle. Stir fry peas, carrots, onion, and chicken until hot and the chicken is no longer pink. Move to the side of the griddle to keep warm. If you have the ability, reduce the temperature on that side of the griddle to medium.
3. Put another tablespoon of oil down and several more shakes of sesame oil. Stir fry cold rice over high heat for 3-4 minutes. Stir in chicken and vegetables.
4. Add soy sauce to taste and stir well. Scoot rice over to one side of griddle and quickly cook the scrambled eggs. Gently mix eggs into rice mixture.
5. Sprinkle the whole thing with MSG and stir, if you are using it.
6. Serve hot.

Nutritional Value (Amount per Serving):

Calories: 571; Fat: 35.08; Carb: 69.34; Protein: 32.2

Blackstone Mexican Fried Rice

Prep Time: 15 minutes   Cook Time: 15 minutes   Serves: 8

Ingredients:

- 6 cups cooked white rice, chilled
- 1/3 cup avocado oil
- 1 cup black beans, drained
- 1 cup corn, drained if using canned
- 1/2 cup diced onion
- 2 cups thinly sliced marinated carne asada (we use pre-marinated carne asada from our local Mexican grocery store)
- 1 can Rotel (or your favorite flavor)
- 1/2 cup salsa or enchilada sauce
- 2 cups shredded Mexican-blend cheese
- 4 tablespoon cilantro

Directions:

1. Preheat your griddle over high heat. Lay down some of the avocado oil in a thin layer.
2. Cook your beans, corn, and onion on one third of the griddle. Flipping occasionally.
3. Put the rice down in a thin layer on another third of the griddle. Let it get a little toasty on the griddle before flipping. Add more oil if necessary.

4. On the last third of the griddle, put down your carne asada meat. Don't flip it until it browns a bit on the bottom!
5. Combine all of the stuff on the grill until it is evenly mixed. Pour over your Rotel on the top, right along with the juice from the can. Add your salsa or enchilada sauce too, and use large spatulas to mix and turn and get all of that juice easily distributed through the rice.
6. Turn the heat down on the griddle and cover with your cheese. Place a cover over and let cook until the cheese is melted.
7. Garnish with cilantro and your favorite taco toppings like sour cream, avocado, diced tomatoes, etc.

Nutritional Value (Amount per Serving):

Calories: 684; Fat: 34.27; Carb: 66.87; Protein: 27.25

Blackstone Steak Fajitas

Prep Time: 30 minutes   Cook Time: 10 minutes   Serves: 12

Ingredients:

- 6 pounds steak
- 2 teaspoons salt
- 1/2 teaspoon pepper
- 2 tablespoons The Spice Guy Fajita seasoning**, divided
- 1 small can El Pato Jalapeno Salsa
- 3 bell peppers, multi-colored
- 1 large onion
- 3 tablespoons avocado oil
- tortillas, of your choice

Directions:

1. Slice your steak into thin strips again the grain. Season with salt, pepper, and 1 1/2 tablespoons of the Fajita seasoning. Place it in a container or plastic baggie. Add in the El Pato Jalapeno Salsa and let sit for 30 minutes.
2. While your steak is sitting, slice your vegetables and season with the remaining Fajita seasoning.
3. Preheat your Blackstone griddle over high heat for 10-15 minutes. Lay down your oil and spread it out evenly before putting down your meat on one side of the griddle and veggies on the other.
4. Cook the steak, flipping occasionally until it is at your desired level of doneness. Remove the vegetables from the griddle when they are still tender-crisp.
5. Heat your tortillas on the griddle briefly before serving with all of your favorite fajita toppings.

Nutritional Value (Amount per Serving):

Calories: 518; Fat: 26.78; Carb: 5.88; Protein: 64.04

Blackstone Duck Fried Rice

Prep Time: 15 minutes   Cook Time: 26 minutes   Serves: 8

Ingredients:

- 4 tablespoons canola oil, divided
- 1 small onion, diced
- 1 teaspoon minced garlic
- 2 duck breasts, diced
- 1 cup frozen peas and carrots
- 3 cups cooked Jasmine rice, chilled
- 2 eggs, lightly beaten
- 1/8 cup soy sauce
- 1 teaspoon sesame oil
- salt and pepper

Directions:

1. Preheat your griddle to medium-high or high heat (basically you just don't want to light the oil on fire), and place about a tablespoon of oil down.
2. Dump on the onions, frozen peas, and carrots and stir fry until heated through and the edges get a little crispy.
3. Add in the duck breast and cook for 2-3 minutes.
4. Move the duck breast and the vegetables over to the side of the griddle that is NOT a hot spot (if your griddle has multiple heat zones, turn one down). If you need to, remove it from the griddle to a pan. Ideally, you want it to stay warm but not continue to cook.
5. Put down some more oil on the griddle and let it heat up. Add on the cold rice and break it apart with your spatula. Continue moving it around the griddle, evenly coating it with oil and letting it get toasty. Add in the garlic during the last minute of cooking. (Add more oil as needed throughout the process.)
6. Combine the duck breast, vegetables, and rice together and stir and toss until they are evenly combined. Drizzle the soy sauce and sesame oil on top and continue to stir and cook until it is evenly distributed.
7. Make a hole in the middle of the rice and add a little more oil. Crack the eggs inside, stir with the spatula, and toss to combine with the rice.

Nutritional Value (Amount per Serving):

Calories: 318; Fat: 21.82; Carb: 26.71; Protein: 17.48

Blackstone Teriyaki Steak Yakisoba

Prep Time: 10 minutes   Cook Time: 15 minutes   Serves: 8

Ingredients:

- 16 ounces fresh steak
- 1 bottle Iron Chef Sesame Garlic sauce

- 4 tablespoons oil
- 1/2 cup sliced onions
- 1 cup asparagus, cut into 1" pieces
- 1 sliced bell pepper
- 1 cup sugar snap pea pods
- 1 cup sliced mushrooms
- 17 ounces fresh yakisoba noodles

Directions:

1. Slice your steaks across the grain, and mix 1/2 of your sauce in. Refrigerate for 4 hours. Slice your onions, peppers, and mushrooms. Get all of your vegetables prepped and ready to go.
2. Preheat your griddle to medium-high heat, place 1 tablespoon of oil on the griddle, add a dash of sesame oil, and quickly stir-fry the vegetables until they are crisp-tender (about 3-4 minutes). Remove from the griddle, cover, and set aside.
3. Preheat another tablespoon of oil on the griddle and add in the noodles. On the other side of the grill, stir fry the steak. Cook for 1-2 minutes, and then combine and toss together with the vegetables.
4. Shut off the heat to the griddle and pour over the remaining sauce. Stir to toss with the noodles, meat, and vegetables.

Nutritional Value (Amount per Serving):

Calories: 285; Fat: 13.8; Carb: 20.8; Protein: 19.71

Ham & Pineapple Fried Rice

Prep Time: 15 minutes   Cook Time: 25 minutes   Serves: 8

Ingredients:

- 4 tablespoons canola oil, divided
- 1 small onion, diced
- 1 cup diced ham
- 1 cup frozen peas and carrots
- 1 cup pineapple chunks
- 3 cups cooked basmati rice, chilled
- 4 eggs, lightly beaten
- 1/4 cup soy sauce
- 1 teaspoon sesame oil
- salt and pepper
- cilantro
- green onion

Directions:

1. Preheat your griddle to medium-high or high heat (basically you just don't want to light the oil on fire), and place about a tablespoon of oil down.
2. Dump on the pineapple, vegetables, and ham on one side of the griddle and stir fry for about 2 minutes.
3. On the other side of the griddle, put down some more oil and let it heat up. Add the cold rice and break it apart with your spatula. Continue moving it around the griddle, evenly coating with oil and letting it get toasty. Add more oil as needed.
4. Combine the meat, vegetables, and rice together and stir and toss until

they are evenly combined.

5. Make a hole in the middle of the rice and add a little more oil. Crack the eggs inside, stir with the spatula, and toss to combine with the rice.
6. Drizzle the soy sauce and sesame oil on top and continue to stir and cook until it is evenly distributed.
7. Top with cilantro and serve hot.

Nutritional Value (Amount per Serving):

Calories: 366; Fat: 24.18; Carb: 35.11; Protein: 16.74

Hibachi-Style Griddle Pork Fried Rice

Prep Time: 15 minutes   Cook Time: 25 minutes   Serves: 8

Ingredients:

- 4 tablespoons canola oil, divided
- 1 small onion, diced
- 1 cup diced Chinese BBQ Pork
- 1 cup frozen peas and carrots
- 3 cups cooked Jasmine rice, chilled
- 2 eggs, lightly beaten
- 1/8 cup soy sauce
- 1 teaspoon sesame oil
- salt and pepper

Directions:

1. Preheat your griddle to medium-high or high heat (basically you just don't want to light the oil on fire), and place about a tablespoon of oil down.
2. Dump on the onions and BBQ pork, and stir fry for about 2 minutes.
3. Add in the frozen peas and carrots and stir fry until heated through and the edges get a little crispy.
4. Move the pork and the vegetables over to the side of the griddle that is NOT a hot spot (if your griddle has multiple heat zones, turn one down).
5. Put down some more oil on the griddle, and let it heat up. Add on the cold rice and break it apart with your spatula. Continue moving it around the griddle, evenly coating with oil and letting it get toasty. Add more oil as needed.
6. Combine the meat, vegetables, and rice together and stir and toss until they are evenly combined. Drizzle the soy sauce and sesame oil on top and continue to stir and cook until it is evenly distributed.
7. Make a hole in the middle of the rice and add a little more oil. Crack the eggs inside, stir with the spatula, and toss to combine with the rice.

Nutritional Value (Amount per Serving):

Calories: 342; Fat: 25.07; Carb: 26.6; Protein: 16.33

Chapter 3: Burgers & Tacos

Blackstone Blackened Fish Tacos

Prep Time: 10 minutes   Cook Time: 8 minutes   Serves: 6

Ingredients:

- 2 pounds white fish (we used lingcod and rockfish)
- 2 tablespoons Blackening seasoning
- 2 teaspoons salt
- 2 tablespoons oil
- 24 corn tortillas
- 2 cups fish taco slaw
- 1 lime, for squeezing

Directions:

1. Preheat your Blackstone over high heat.
2. Pat your fresh fish fillets dry and then generously season with the Blackening seasoning and the salt.
3. Put the oil down on the griddle and put the fish on top of the oil.
4. Lay out all the tortillas on the griddle to warm also, if there's room on your griddle.
5. Flip the fish after about 4 minutes, and cook for an additional 3-4 minutes on the other side. (If your fish is less than 3/4"-1" thick, it'll take less time to cook. Keep that in mind!)
6. Remove from the griddle and load into your tortillas. Top with the fish slaw and enjoy while hot with limes for squeezing.

Nutritional Value (Amount per Serving):

Calories: 1055; Fat: 83.45; Carb: 45.12; Protein: 30.97

Blackstone Tacos Borrachos

Prep Time: 10 minutes   Cook Time: 8 minutes   Serves: 6

Ingredients:

- 2 pounds flank steak
- 1 onion, chopped
- 3 cloves garlic, chopped
- 1/4 cup chopped cilantro
- 12 ounces beer
- 2 tablespoons Spanglish Asadero All-Purpose Rub
- 1 lime, juiced
- 2 tablespoons avocado oil
- 24 corn tortillas

Garnish

- Onions, finely diced
- Cilantro, chopped
- 6 ounces Cotija cheese, crumbled
- Hot Sauce

Directions:

1. Place your flank steak, onion, garlic, cilantro, and the beer into a large freezer baggie or storage container. Let it marinate for 4 hours.
2. Preheat your griddle over high heat.
3. Drain off the marinade and pat the meat dry.
4. Slice the steak against the grain into thin strips. As thin as you can slice them. Just shy of shaved.
5. Season all over with the Spanglish Asadero rub (or your favorite Mexican rub will work too!) Squeeze the lime over the meat.
6. Put the avocado oil down on the hot griddle and let it get hot too.
7. Add the meat to the griddle and let it brown on one side before stirring. Then flip and stir until it is no longer pink.
8. Heat the tortillas on the griddle before loading them up with steak, chopped onions, cilantro, and your favorite hot sauce.

Nutritional Value (Amount per Serving):

Calories: 692; Fat: 30.58; Carb: 56.74; Protein: 47.88

Smash Burger Tacos

Prep Time: 10 minutes   Cook Time: 15 minutes   Serves: 6

Ingredients:

- 2 pounds 80/20 Ground Sirloin or Chuck
- Salt, Pepper, Garlic powder
- 1/2 medium onion, sliced
- 6 corn tortillas
- 6 slices cheddar cheese
- 1 cup lettuce
- 2 tomatoes, sliced
- 24 slices dill pickles
- 3 tablespoons thousand island dressing

Directions:

1. Preheat your griddle to medium-high heat.
2. Divide your burger into 6 equally sized balls.
3. Smash each ball with a large spatula or a burger smasher until it is about 1/4" thick.

4. Let the burger develop a nice crust on the bottom. Season the top with salt, pepper, and garlic powder. Flip the burger and immediately put a tortilla on top of the cooked side of the burger.
5. Put the onions down on the griddle and let them cook in the burger grease. Flip occasionally and let them brown.
6. Let the other side of the burger develop a crust. Flip the whole thing over, and let the tortilla crisp on the griddle surface. Add cheese on top and cover. Cook until the cheese is melted and the tortilla is crispy.
7. Top each "taco" with your lettuce, tomato, pickles, grilled onions, and thousand island dressing.
8. Enjoy!

Nutritional Value (Amount per Serving):

Calories: 413; Fat: 22.7; Carb: 14.63; Protein: 38.35

Quadruple Smash Burger

Prep Time: 5 minutes   Cook Time: 20 minutes   Serves: 4

Ingredients:

- 4 pounds lean ground beef
- salt and pepper

Fixings

- 16 dill pickle chips
- 1 small onions, diced
- 4 slices tomato

- 20 slices American cheese
- 4 hamburger buns

- 4 slices leaf lettuce
- 4 tablespoons ketchup
- 4 teaspoons mustard

Directions:

1. Form the burger into 20 equally-sized balls. They should be around 3 ounces each. Season the tops of each patty lightly with salt and pepper.
2. Preheat your griddle or flat top or cast iron over medium-high to high heat.
3. Place the burger balls onto the grill, one at a time, and immediately smash them down with a burger smasher, bacon press, or heavy-duty spatula.
4. Cook for several minutes until a dark-brown crust forms, season the uncooked side of the burger, and then flip.
5. Toast your buns.
6. Top each patty with a slice of cheese, cover with a melting dome (if necessary), and cook another couple of minutes until the bottom also has the crust formed.
7. Remove from the flat top, load up 5 patties to a bun, and serve hot!

Nutritional Value (Amount per Serving):

Calories: 1872; Fat: 102.48; Carb: 64.75; Protein: 166.86

Blackstone Pulled Pork Tacos

Prep Time: 15 minutes   Cook Time: 12 minutes   Serves: 8

Ingredients:

- 24 corn tortillas
- avocado oil
- 6 cups shredded Mexican-blend cheese
- 6 cups cooked shredded pulled pork
- taco toppings

Directions:

1. Preheat the griddle to medium-low heat for 10-15 minutes.
2. Lay down the tortillas and cover with cheese.
3. Spread the meat over half of the tortilla, fold over the other half, and cook for 3-4 minutes per side, or until both sides are browned and crisp.
4. Serve hot with all your favorite taco fixings!

Nutritional Value (Amount per Serving):

Calories: 632; Fat: 32.52; Carb: 34.88; Protein: 49.65

Ultimate Bacon Onion Smash Burger

Prep Time: 5 minutes   Cook Time: 20 minutes   Serves: 8

Ingredients:

- 3 pounds ground beef
- salt and pepper
- 8 slices thick-cut bacon

Bacon-Wrapped Onions

- 8 slices onions

- 8 slices cheese
- 8 hamburger buns

- 16 slices thin bacon

Directions:

1. Slice your onion into thick, 1/2" - 3/4" slices.
2. Form the burgers into 8 equally-sized balls. Season the tops with salt and pepper.
3. Preheat your griddle or flat top or cast iron over medium-high to high heat.
4. Place the burger balls onto the grill, and immediately smash down with a burger smasher, bacon press, or heavy-duty spatula.
5. Cook for several minutes until a dark-brown crust forms, season the uncooked side of the burger, and then flip.
6. Top with cheese, cover with a melting lid (if necessary), and cook another couple of minutes until the bottom also has the crust formed.
7. Remove from the flat top and serve hot!

Nutritional Value (Amount per Serving):

Calories: 1216; Fat: 83.27; Carb: 37.82; Protein: 76.82

Blackstone Bacon Cheeseburger

Prep Time: 10 minutes   Cook Time: 15 minutes   Serves: 6

Ingredients:

- 3 pounds ground waygu beef
- salt and pepper
- 12 pieces Kurobuta bacon
- 6 slices aged sharp cheddar
- 6 brioche buns
- toppings of your choosing

Directions:

1. Preheat your griddle for 10-15 minutes over medium heat.
2. While the griddle is preheating, form your burger into 6 patties that are slightly larger than your buns, and have a depression in the middle.
3. Season both sides of the patties with salt and pepper.
4. Cook the bacon and toast your buns. If your griddle is big enough, you can start the burgers after your bacon is about halfway cooked.
5. Cook the burgers for about 4-5 minutes a side, or until they are at least 145°F for medium-rare or 160°F for medium. (if you are using a high-quality burger it is okay to cook it to this temp, but if you are at risk for food-borne illness complications, proceed with caution.)
6. During the last 3 minutes of cooking, top the burgers with the cheese slices and cover with a large dome to melt.
7. Build, top with your favorite condiments, and serve!

Nutritional Value (Amount per Serving):

Calories: 1171; Fat: 77.69; Carb: 39.42; Protein: 70.39

Blackstone Fish Tacos with Peach Salsa

Prep Time: 10 minutes   Cook Time: 15 minutes   Serves: 6

Ingredients:

- 1 1/2 pound white fish (we used Cobia)
- 4 tablespoons butter
- 1 tablespoon olive oil
- 1 teaspoon salt
- 1/2 teaspoon pepper
- 1/2 teaspoon granulated garlic
- 1/2 teaspoon onion powder

- 1 tablespoon sugar
- 2 ounces Triple Sec orange liqueur
- 2 ounces orange juice

Garnish
- Shredded cabbage
- hot sauce
- cilantro (if desired)

Directions:

1. Rinse off your fish with cold water and pat dry with paper towels.
2. Cut the fish into 3/4" cubes.
3. Season well with the salt, pepper, garlic powder, and onion powder.
4. Place the seasoned fish cubes into a bowl and toss with the olive oil until they are evenly coated.
5. Preheat your flat top griddle over medium to medium-high heat and put some butter down in the middle of the griddle. When it begins to bubble, spread your fish out over the butter.
6. Let the butter brown the bottom of the fish and then flip once, after about 1 or 2 minutes.
7. Sprinkle the sugar on top of the fish immediately after flipping, and let it cook for another 1 or 2 minutes before turning again.
8. Pour the orange liqueur and the orange juice over the fish, cover with a melting dome, and let cook for one more minute.
9. Remove from the grill and pile into tortillas.
10. Top with shredded cabbage, your favorite hot sauce, and heaps of the peach salsa in the recipe below.

Nutritional Value (Amount per Serving):

Calories: 215; Fat: 12.64; Carb: 5.46; Protein: 19.67

Traeger Beef Birria Tacos

Prep Time: 15 minutes   Cook Time: 5 hours   Serves: 8

Ingredients:

Meat
- 4 pounds beef chuck shoulder roast
- 4 tablespoons Mexican seasoning blend
- 1 teaspoon salt
- 1 teaspoon pepper

Consommé / braising liquid
- 12 dried guajillo peppers, seeds and stems removed
- 1 teaspoon salt

- 1/4 teaspoon ground cloves
- 1 teaspoon thyme
- 1/2 teaspoon cumin
- 1 teaspoon peppercorns
- 1 teaspoon cayenne or habanero powder (optional)
- 1 tablespoon Mexican oregano
- 5 cloves garlic
- 1 large onion, halved
- 1 15 ounce can whole plum or roma tomatoes
- 6 cups water
- 2 cups beef broth (optional)

Tacos
- 24 corn tortillas
- 6 cups shredded Mexican-blend cheese
- diced onion
- cilantro

Directions:

Brown & smoke the meat
1. Turn on your pellet grill to "smoke" at 220°F.
2. Season your beef with the Mexican seasoning blend and the salt and pepper.
3. Smoke for 2-3 hours.

Make the consommé
1. Remove the stem and seeds from the peppers and place them into a pot with the rest of the ingredients for the consommé. Bring up to a simmer, and let cook for 10-15 minutes.
2. Remove from heat and let cool for 15-20 minutes.
3. Blend until smooth, and set aside.

Braise the meat
1. Place the meat into a slow cooker, Instant Pot, or Dutch Oven. Strain the blended consommé mixture through a fine mesh strainer. If the liquid doesn't cover the beef, pour in some beef broth until there's enough to cover.
2. Let braise over low heat for 2-3 hours, minimum, or until the meat is tender and shreddable.
3. Shred, removing any unappetizing bits, and reserve the consommé.

Fire up the flat top or non-stick pan on the stove
1. Preheat your Blackstone over medium-low heat.
2. While it is heating, dip your corn tortillas in the consommé and place on the flat top griddle. Top the whole tortilla with cheese, and half of it with some shredded beef. You can also add onions and cilantro at this stage if you want.

3. Fold over the empty half of the tortilla and lightly press down. Cook for an additional 2-4 minutes and flip. Continue cooking until the other side is crisp and then remove from the griddle.
4. Repeat until all of the tacos are cooked. You can keep them hot in a foil pan held on one part of the griddle and covered with foil over low heat.

EAT!

1. Serve the tacos with any kind of fixing you like and a small dish of the consommé for dipping.

Nutritional Value (Amount per Serving):

Calories: 1012; Fat: 46.02; Carb: 65.79; Protein: 87.4

Blackstone Fish Tacos with Peach Salsa

Prep Time: 15 minutes   Cook Time: 5 minutes   Serves: 6

Ingredients:

Shrimp Tacos
- 1 pound peeled and deveined shrimp
- 1 tablespoon cajun blackening seasoning
- 1/2 teaspoon salt
- 1/4 teaspoon cayenne pepper
- 1 cup shredded green cabbage
- 1-2 tablespoons avocado oil
- 8 medium-sized flour tortillas

Directions:

1. Preheat your Blackstone on medium heat.
2. Season your shrimp with the blackening seasoning, salt, and cayenne.
3. Cook the shrimp for 3-4 minutes, or until they are no longer translucent and they have turned pink.
4. Remove from the griddle, and toss on the tortillas to give them a quick warm-up, and then stuff them with shrimp, cabbage, strawberry salsa, and whatever hot sauce you want to be brave enough to throw on top.

Nutritional Value (Amount per Serving):

Calories: 305; Fat: 8.71; Carb: 34.33; Protein: 20.8

Blackstone Mushroom and Swiss Burger

Prep Time: 10 minutes   Cook Time: 10 minutes   Serves: 6

Ingredients:

- 2 pounds ground beef
- 6 ounces mushrooms sliced
- 2 tablespoons butter
- 1 teaspoon garlic salt

- 1 teaspoon pepper
- 6 slices Swiss cheese
- 6 hamburger buns

Directions:

1. Preheat the Blackstone Grill over medium high heat (approximately 400 degrees F).
2. Add the butter to the grill and spread it out with a spatula.
3. Add the sliced mushrooms to the grill and season it with half the garlic salt. Toss to sauté the mushrooms in the butter and garlic salt.
4. Divide the ground beef into 6 even balls (approximately 1/3 pound each).
5. Place the ground beef on the Blackstone grill next to the mushrooms.
6. Press firmly on the ground beef balls into the Blackstone Grill. Do not smash it all the way down but just press slightly to form a burger patty.
7. Season the beef with the remaining garlic salt and pepper.
8. Cook the patties for 3-5 minutes until the sides of the patties begin to change colors.
9. Flip the burgers (do not smash them down) and cook until burgers are cooked through (3-4 more minutes).
10. Top each patties with the cooked sliced mushrooms and a piece of the Swiss cheese. Allow the cheese to melt onto the patties (1-2 minutes).
11. Remove the beef and add them to one of the hamburger buns.
12. Then add your favorite burger toppings and enjoy!

Nutritional Value (Amount per Serving):

Calories: 872; Fat: 51.26; Carb: 39.93; Protein: 61.97

Chapter 4: Vegetable & Side

Blackstone Pierogies

Prep Time: 5 minutes   Cook Time: 20 minutes   Serves: 6

Ingredients:

- 4 tablespoons butter
- 4 slices bacon
- 1 shallot
- 12 Potato and Cheese Pierogi, fresh or thawed
- 1/2 cup sour cream
- 1 tablespoon chopped chives

Directions:

1. Preheat your griddle over medium heat.
2. Slice the shallot into rounds and chop the bacon into small pieces.
3. Place both on the griddle to cook.
4. Melt some butter on the other half of the griddle and put your pierogies down. Let them brown on one side before flipping and browning on the other side.
5. Stir and flip the bacon and shallots as needed until the bacon is crisp and the shallots are lightly browned.
6. Serve the pierogies with the bacon and shallots on top and a generous serving of sour cream. Sprinkle with your chopped chives and serve hot.

Nutritional Value (Amount per Serving):

Calories: 734; Fat: 17.19; Carb: 130.74; Protein: 17.89

Marinated Sauteed Mushrooms

Prep Time: 10 minutes   Cook Time: 5 minutes   Serves: 6

Ingredients:

- 4 ounces mushrooms
- 1 tablespoon red wine vinegar
- 1/4 teaspoon salt
- 1/4 teaspoon pepper
- 2 tablespoons butter

Directions:

1. Separate the mushrooms, if necessary. Sprinkle with salt and pepper and pour the red wine vinegar over the top. Stir until most of the liquid has been absorbed.
2. Preheat your cast-iron pan or Blackstone griddle over medium heat. Place the butter into the hot pan and let it melt. As soon as it is melted, pour the mushrooms onto the cooking surface.
3. Let the mushrooms cook for 2-3 minutes, covered. Remove the cover and

stir. Cook an additional 2-3 minutes, covered.

4. Remove and serve hot.

Nutritional Value (Amount per Serving):

Calories: 91; Fat: 4.03; Carb: 14.43; Protein: 1.89

Togarashi Zucchini Noodles

Prep Time: 16 minutes   Cook Time: 5 minutes   Serves: 6

Ingredients:

- 2 medium zucchini
- 1/2 cup canola oil
- 1/4 cup bacon grease
- 1-2 tablespoons togarashi seasoning

Directions:

1. Preheat your Blackstone to medium heat for 10-15 minutes.
2. Place some bacon grease and oil down on the griddle.
3. Spiralize the zucchini following the package directions, quickly cook it in the hot oil for 2 minutes. Sprinkle with half the togarashi. Remove to a plate covered with paper towels. Sprinkle with the remaining togarashi seasoning. Taste, and add salt if necessary.

Nutritional Value (Amount per Serving):

Calories: 245; Fat: 26.74; Carb: 1.35; Protein: 0.2

Blackstone Italian Dunkers

Prep Time: 10 minutes   Cook Time: 10 minutes   Serves: 6

Ingredients:

- 1 loaf Italian (or French) bread
- 1 stick salted butter
- 2 tablespoons Johnny's Garlic Bread Seasoning
- 1 cup shredded Parmesan cheese
- 2 cups shredded mozzarella cheese (optional, and not included in photos)
- 1 pound ground beef
- 1 teaspoon salt, pepper, garlic blend (or approximately 1/3 teaspoon of each to add up to 1 teaspoon if you don't have a blend.)
- 1 48-ounce jar marinara

Directions:

1. Slice the bread into rounds. Combine the butter and Garlic Bread

seasoning, and spread over both the front and the back of the cuts.

2. Preheat the Blackstone over low heat. You want to run it around 325°F-ish for the best results.

3. Cook the ground beef over medium heat. Season with the SPG. Place the cooked ground beef into a saucepan and top with the marinara sauce. Place the pan on the griddle to heat while you are toasting your garlic bread.

4. Toast each side of the garlic bread until golden brown. If desired, top with cheese(s) and cover or pop into an oven under a broiler for a minute until it is melted and bubbly.

5. Serve the toasted garlic bread with the meaty marinade for dipping!

Nutritional Value (Amount per Serving):

Calories: 696; Fat: 28.86; Carb: 60.49; Protein: 46.32

Smoked Beef Pancit

Prep Time: 20 minutes   Cook Time: 4 hours   Serves: 10

Ingredients:

- 2 pounds whole beef sirloin roast
- 1 tablespoon OWYD Everything rub (or your favorite beef rub)
- 16 ounces rice vermicelli noodles

Vegetables
- 8 ounces green cabbage
- 2 whole carrots
- 2 green onions

Sauce
- 1/4 cup soy sauce
- 1 cup beef stock
- 1 tablespoon sugar
- 1/2 teaspoon black pepper

Directions:

1. Preheat your grill to 225°F. Rub the beef, and place onto the grill. Cook for 3-4 hours, or until the roast is probe-tender and in the 198-202°F range. If the roast stalls along the way, you can wrap it and continue cooking to speed things along.

2. Soak the noodles. 10 minutes in HOT water usually does the trick. They'll finish cooking on the griddle.

3. While the noodles soak, slice the green onions (greens AND white parts), cabbage, and carrots. Set aside. Mix together the soy sauce, beef stock, sugar, and black pepper and set aside.

4. Preheat your griddle over medium heat and double-check that your prep

work is done and you have EVERYTHING you need. You can't walk away from stir fry on the Blackstone while it is cooking. Don't forget the serving tray to put the food on when it is done.

5. Place the carrots and cabbage down on the griddle with a few tablespoons of oil. Season with some salt and pepper and cook for 2 minutes, stirring often.
6. Move the vegetables to a cool part of the griddle, place some more oil down and then add the drained vermicelli noodles.
7. Pour over the sauce over the noodles, little bits at a time, adding more when what is down gets soaked up into the noodles. Add in the sliced green onions.
8. On another part of the griddle, stir fry the smoked beef briefly until it is heated through, and then mix the vegetables and meat together.
9. Move the whole thing to a serving plate and enjoy!

Nutritional Value (Amount per Serving):

Calories: 243; Fat: 11.03; Carb: 8.95; Protein: 25.71

Blackstone Marinated Portabella Mushrooms

Prep Time: 35 minutes   Cook Time: 5 minutes   Serves: 4

Ingredients:

- 2 large portobello mushrooms
- 2 tablespoons olive oil
- 1 tablespoon red wine vinegar
- 1 tablespoon cherry blossom shoyu
- 1/4 teaspoon salt
- 1/4 teaspoon pepper
- 1 tablespoon butter

Directions:

1. Cut the stems off of the mushrooms and then scrape all of the gills out from under the cap.
2. Drizzle with olive oil on both the top and the bottom of the mushroom cap, and then place top-down before sprinkling with salt, pepper, vinegar, and shoyu.
3. Cover, and let marinate in the fridge for about 30 minutes.
4. Carefully place the mushrooms onto the griddle that's been preheated to medium-high, taking care not to spill out the marinade.
5. Place the butter between the caps and cover. Let cook for four minutes.
6. Remove the cover and cook for an additional minute.
7. Cut the caps into slices using a knife or bench scraper. The marinade will spill out onto the griddle and create a big of a sauce. Cook for another minute, and then remove from the griddle and scrape up any sauce you can, if desired.

8. Eat!

Nutritional Value (Amount per Serving):

Calories: 96; Fat: 9.8; Carb: 1.87; Protein: 1.04

Fried Wontons

Prep Time: 15 minutes   Cook Time: 5 minutes   Serves: 6

Ingredients:

- 24 wonton wrappers
- 1/2 pound ground chicken
- 1 teaspoon minced garlic
- 1/2 teaspoon minced ginger
- 1 tablespoon soy sauce
- 2 teaspoons togarashi
- oil for frying

Directions:

1. Combine the chicken, garlic, ginger, soy sauce, and togarashi in a small bowl, and mix to combine.
2. Stuff about a tablespoon into each wrapper, brush the edges with water, and then fold into a triangle. Fold the edges in toward the middle, and set aside.
3. Preheat 1 or1 1/2 inches of oil in a skillet over medium to medium-high heat.
4. Fry the wontons in batches, flipping once until both sides are golden brown. They should fry for 3-4 minutes. If they are getting done sooner than that, turn your oil down a bit. You need to give them enough time to fully cook the filling.
5. Remove to a separate plate and serve with vinegar soy dipping sauce.

Nutritional Value (Amount per Serving):

Calories: 442; Fat: 6.22; Carb: 74.97; Protein: 19.36

Griddle Chicken Kabobs with Vegetables

Prep Time: 2-9 hours   Cook Time: 25 minutes   Serves: 6

Ingredients:

- Chicken Breast, Boneless & Skinless 2 each
- Olive Oil 1/4 cup
- Ranch Seasoning Packet 1 ounce
- Mushrooms, White, Sliced 8 ounces
- Onion, White, Small Pieces 1 Each
- Pepper, Bell, Small Pieces 1 Each

Directions:

1. Gather your ingredients to make the chicken vegetable kabobs.
2. Cut the boneless, skinless chicken breast into one-inch cubes trying to keep them the same size.
3. In a medium bowl, add the chicken pieces and sprinkle the ranch powdered seasoning packet on top of the chicken.
4. Pour the olive oil over the chicken/ranch mixture and stir to combine all the ingredients.
5. Cover the container and refrigerate for 1 - 8 hours. When ready to make the kabobs, remove from the fridge.
6. Gather all your skewer ingredients and line them up on the countertop.
7. Take a skewer and start with a piece of onion. Poke the skewer in the center of the onion piece, being careful to not poke your hand, and slide the vegetable piece all the way to the other end.
8. Next, add a piece of the marinated chicken breast through the center and slide it to touch the vegetable piece. Add a piece of the other remaining vegetables.
9. Repeat this assembly process several more times until your skewer is full. I was able to get two chicken vegetable kabobs per chicken breast.
10. Preheat your Blackstone Griddle on the low setting. Add a layer of oil to the flat top griddle.
11. Place the skewers on the flat top and cook the chicken kabobs, low and slow so that you do not burn. Cover with a dome lid.
12. Let the chicken skewers cook until the first side is golden brown. With a pair of tongs, carefully flip the kabob to the opposite side. Replace the cover over the skewers. Continue cooking until that side is golden brown. Flip again to a non-grilled side and continue cooking until all four sides are golden brown in color and the chicken is completely cooked and reached a temperature of 165°F.
13. Griddle chicken kabobs cooked on the low setting will take about 20-25 minutes but cooking times will vary. Make sure to test one of the middle pieces of chicken breast on the skewer for doneness. The skewer should be a golden-brown color, not burnt black.

Nutritional Value (Amount per Serving):

Calories: 264; Fat: 18; Carb: 3.71; Protein: 20.81

Blackstone Griddle Spicy Beef Lettuce Wraps

Prep Time: 20 minutes   Cook Time: 10 minutes   Serves: 4

Ingredients:

Sauce
- 2 chile peppers hot, finely chopped
- 1/2 teaspoon sugar
- 2 tablespoons fish sauce
- 4 scallions thinly sliced
- 2 limes juiced

Wrap
- 1 pound ground beef
- 4 tablespoons fresh cilantro chopped
- 8 lettuce leaves
- avocado oil for cooking

Directions:

1. Preheat the griddle at medium heat. If using a thermometer, you'll want it at about 375-400°F.
2. While griddle is preheating, combine all the sauce ingredients in a small bowl and whisk to dissolve the sugar.
3. When the griddle is hot, drizzle a little avocado oil and add the ground beef. Let it cook undisturbed for a couple of minutes, then flip and start breaking it up with your spatula. Cook until most of the pink is gone, which should take about 5-7 minutes total.
4. Pour the sauce over the ground beef and toss to combine. Cook for about a minute or two to thicken the sauce slightly and to soften the onions.
5. Serve in lettuce wraps. Top with extra cilantro or green onions if desired.

Nutritional Value (Amount per Serving):

Calories: 379; Fat: 26.84; Carb: 3.14; Protein: 30.18

Smashed Potatoes with Tapenade

Prep Time: 15 minutes   Cook Time: 25 minutes   Serves: 4

Ingredients:

For the tapenade
- 1cup Kalamata olives, minced
- 2tablespoons capers, rinsed and minced
- 1teaspoon grated lemon zest
- 1tablespoon fresh lemon juice
- 11/2teaspoons fresh thyme, chopped
- 1/2cup extra virgin olive oil
- Freshly ground black pepper

For the potatoes
- 4 red or white potatoes, about 5 ounces each, well-scrubbed
- 2 tablespoons red wine vinegar

- 1 bay leaf
- 6 black peppercorns
- Salt

Directions:

1. In a bowl, combine all ingredients for tapenade. May be refrigerated up to one week in a tightly sealed container.
2. Put potatoes in a saucepan with vinegar, bay leaf, peppercorns, salt and water to cover. Bring to a boil, then reduce heat and continue to cook for 12 to 15 minutes, until potatoes are soft. Drain. While still warm, place potatoes in a dishtowel and gently crush with the flat of your hand on a hard surface.
3. Heat a seasoned griddle over medium-low grill or stovetop until a drop of water sizzles on surface. Place potatoes on griddle and cook without moving until golden brown, about 5 minutes. Remove potatoes to a plate with a wide spatula. Top uncooked side with 2 tablespoons tapenade, pressing it into potato. Put potatoes back on griddle, tapenade side down, and cook another 5 minutes. Serve immediately.

Nutritional Value (Amount per Serving):

Calories: 215; Fat: 18.47; Carb: 10.42; Protein: 3.08

Candied Sweet Potatoes

Prep Time: 10 minutes   Cook Time: 15 minutes   Serves: 4

Ingredients:

- 3 medium sweet potatoes
- 2 tablespoons cooking oil or substitute beef tallow
- 3 tablespoons butter
- 1/2 teaspoon ground cinnamon
- 1/3 cup brown sugar loosely packed
- 3-4 tablespoons maple syrup
- 1 teaspoon fresh rosemary chopped

Directions:

1. Preheat griddle on low. While griddle is heating up, peel and cut sweet potatoes into cubes about 3/4" in size.
2. Add about 2 tablespoons of your favorite cooking oil or beef tallow to the warm griddle surface. Add the cut sweet potatoes to the oil and gently toss to combine. Allow the sweet potatoes to cook in the oil for about 3-4 minutes.
3. Add about 2-3 tablespoons of water on or near the sweet potatoes to create steam. Place a metal melting dome over the sweet potatoes and allow them

to steam for about 4-5 minutes, or until about 80-90% done. About every minute while the sweet potatoes are steaming, carefully remove the dome to stir the potatoes.

4. When sweet potatoes are almost done, remove the dome and allow them to cook uncovered until tender and done to your liking.

5. Add butter, cinnamon, brown sugar, and syrup to the potatoes. Gently toss to combine all ingredients, and cook for an additional 1-2 minutes, stirring frequently.

6. Add fresh rosemary to the candied sweet potatoes and stir to combine. When sauce is reduced (should take about 2 minutes) transfer candied sweet potatoes to a serving dish and serve warm.

Nutritional Value (Amount per Serving):

Calories: 299; Fat: 15.22; Carb: 40.34; Protein: 1.67

Bacon-Fried Corn

Prep Time: 10 minutes   Cook Time: 10 minutes   Serves: 4

Ingredients:

- 1 pound bacon chopped into 1/2-inch thick pieces
- 4 cups corn kernels from fresh or frozen
- 2 tablespoons minced garlic about 3 cloves
- 1/2 cup sliced green onions white and green parts
- 1/2 teaspoon paprika
- 2 tablespoons chopped parsley
- salt and pepper to taste

Directions:

1. Preheat your Blackstone griddle, or other outdoor flattop griddle, to medium-high.

2. Slice and cook the bacon until it starts to get crispy. Push it to the side to continue cooking.

3. Add the corn kernels right on top of where you cooked the bacon, so they soak up all the bacon fat and bits.

4. Cook the corn over medium-high for 2-3 minutes, then add the garlic and cook an additional minute.

5. Add the green onions to the corn mixture, then work the bacon back into the corn.

6. Season with paprika, and salt and pepper to taste.

7. Serve and enjoy!

Nutritional Value (Amount per Serving):

Calories: 525; Fat: 37.15; Carb: 43.24; Protein: 17.36

Chapter 5: Fish & Seafood

Blackstone Sweet Chili Shrimp

Prep Time: 30-60 minutes   Cook Time: 10 minutes   Serves: 4

Ingredients:

- 2 pounds raw colossal shrimp

Marinade

- 1 tablespoon honey
- 1 teaspoon granulated garlic
- 1 teaspoon onion powder
- 1/2 teaspoon salt
- 1/4 teaspoon black pepper
- 1 teaspoon red pepper flakes

- 1 tablespoon garlic chili sauce
- 1 tablespoon brown sugar
- 1 tablespoon rice vinegar
- 3 tablespoons soy sauce
- 2 tablespoons oil

Sauce

- 1/2 cup Sweet Chili Sauce

Directions:

1. Mix all the marinade ingredients. Toss with the shrimp and let marinate in the fridge for 30-60 minutes.
2. Preheat the griddle over medium heat.
3. Lay down a thin layer of oil.
4. Dump the shrimp and marinade out onto the griddle.
5. Cook for a couple of minutes per side. The internal temperature of the shrimp should be 120°F-125°F.
6. Enjoy! Eat them as peel-and-eat shrimp or remove the shells, add some extra sweet chili sauce, and serve over rice.

Nutritional Value (Amount per Serving):

Calories: 400; Fat: 12.2; Carb: 20.3; Protein: 48.49

Blackstone Meat Church Shrimp Fajitas

Prep Time: 5 minutes   Cook Time: 5 minutes   Serves: 6

Ingredients:

- 2 pounds shrimp
- 2 tablespoons Meat Church Fajita Rub
- 1 lime
- 1 red bell pepper
- 1 medium yellow onion
- 1 yellow bell pepper

Fixings

- 12 tortillas

- lettuce
- sour cream
- hot sauce
- avocado

Directions:

1. Preheat your Blackstone to medium-high heat.
2. Prep your vegetables by slicing into strips and discarding stems and seeds from the peppers.
3. Make sure your shrimp have no shells or tails. Toss them in a squeeze of lime juice and coat well with the seasoning rub.
4. Cook the vegetables on one half of the grill. The vegetables take longer than the shrimp, but still only take about 3-4 minutes.
5. Place the shrimp on the grill and cook for about a minute per side. You want the shrimp to be pink, but don't overcook them!
6. Load up into tortillas (heat them up on the griddle too for bonus points, or use the fresh, uncooked tortillas available in most grocery stores now).

Nutritional Value (Amount per Serving):

Calories: 540; Fat: 16.16; Carb: 56.69; Protein: 40.6

Miso Marinated Black Cod

Prep Time: 5 minutes   Cook Time: 8 minutes   Serves: 8

Ingredients:

- 4 8-ounce Black Cod filets
- 1/3 cup white miso
- 1/4 cup sake
- 3 tablespoons Mirin
- 2 tablespoons sugar in the raw
- 2 tablespoons shoyu soy sauce
- 1 tablespoon oil

Directions:

1. Wash and pat dry your fish filets. Mix together the white miso, sake, mirin, sugar, and soy sauce. Place the marinade and the fish into a sealable baggie and refrigerate for at least 4 hours.
2. Remove the fish from the marinade and rinse off the excess marinade and pat dry with paper towels.
3. Preheat your cast iron pan or Blackstone griddle over medium heat. You want the surface temperature to be around 350°F.
4. Put a thin layer of oil into the pan or onto the griddle, and cook the fish for about 3 minutes per side. 145°F is the official USDA safe temp for fish. We like ours more around 135°F.
5. Serve over rice with a drizzle of soy glaze or soy sauce and sriracha.

Nutritional Value (Amount per Serving):

Calories: 136; Fat: 2.87; Carb: 5.56; Protein: 19

Blackstone Air Fryer Lobster Tails

Prep Time: 10 minutes   Cook Time: 7 minutes   Serves: 6

Ingredients:

- 6 lobster tails, split
- 1 teaspoon salt
- 1 teaspoon paprika
- 1 teaspoon Old Bay
- 1/2 teaspoon pepper
- 6 tablespoons smoked garlic butter (or some salted butter with garlic powder also works in a pinch)

Directions:

1. Halve the lobster tails by down the middle with kitchen shears or a sharp knife. Alternatively, you can also butterfly the lobster tail by cutting down the middle top of the shell, pulling it apart, separate the meat from the shell, and close the shell under the meat so it is resting on top.
2. Brush the meat with garlic butter and season with salt, paprika, Old Bay, and pepper.
3. Preheat your air fryer to 450°F (or "high" if yours doesn't go all the way to 450°F).
4. Place the lobster tails in, meat-side-up, and cook for 5-7 minutes.
5. Remove, brush with more garlic butter (if desired), and serve hot.

Nutritional Value (Amount per Serving):

Calories: 55; Fat: 0.4; Carb: 11.05; Protein: 2.83

Blackstone Crab Scampi

Prep Time: 10 minutes   Cook Time: 15 minutes   Serves: 6

Ingredients:

- 6 pounds pre-cooked crab
- 1 cup melted salted butter
- 2 teaspoons kosher salt
- 1 tablespoon Old Bay seasoning blend
- 2 tablespoons minced garlic
- 1 cup dry white wine

Directions:

1. Preheat your griddle over medium heat.
2. Place the crab on the griddle and season with the salt and Old Bay and toss to coat. Spoon on the garlic, and then drizzle with butter. Cook for a minute, using the tons to move the crabs and garlic butter around on the griddle.
3. Pour the wine over crab, cover, and let steam for 2-3 minutes.
4. Using a bench scraper, keep scraping and spooning the wine/garlic/butter sauce over the top of the crabs.
5. Remove and serve hot!

Nutritional Value (Amount per Serving):

Calories: 2075; Fat: 194.81; Carb: 1.64; Protein: 74.69

Blackstone Shrimp Fajitas

Prep Time: 10 minutes   Cook Time: 10 minutes   Serves: 6

Ingredients:

- avocado oil
- 1 green pepper
- 1 yellow pepper
- 1 red pepper
- 1 medium yellow onion
- 3 pounds large raw shrimp (washed, peeled, and deveined)

Pre-made seasoning

- 2 tablespoons Spiceology Chile Margarita

Or use this homemade seasoning

- 1 teaspoon chili powder
- 1/2 teaspoon garlic powder
- 1/2 teaspoon onion powder
- 1/2 teaspoon salt
- 1/4 teaspoon cumin

Directions:

1. Mix the seasoning mix together and sprinkle evenly over the shrimp and vegetables.
2. Preheat your griddle over medium-high heat and lay down a bit of avocado oil.
3. Pour the shrimp and vegetables on the griddle and let sizzle for about 1-2 minutes.
4. Flip everything over with giant spatulas and cook until the shrimp is pink and the vegetables are crisp-tender.

5. Serve with your favorite fixings and warm tortillas.

Nutritional Value (Amount per Serving):

Calories: 91; Fat: 4.42; Carb: 11.6; Protein: 2.43

Salmon Filet

Prep Time: 10 minutes   Cook Time:8 minutes   Serves: 4

Ingredients:

- 1/4 cup soy sauce or gluten-free tamari
- 1/4 cup oil like avocado oil
- 2 tablespoons brown sugar
- 1 teaspoon dried basil
- 1 teaspoon dried thyme
- 1 teaspoon garlic powder.
- 1/4 teaspoon sea salt
- 1/4 teaspoon fresh ground black pepper
- 16 ounces salmon filets
- Oil for the griddle
- For serving: Freshly squeezed lemon juice

Directions:

1. In a medium bowl, whisk together the soy sauce, avocado oil, brown sugar, basil, thyme, garlic powder, salt, and pepper.
2. Place the fish in a zip-top bag or shallow dish and pour the marinade over it.
3. Refrigerate for 1 hour.

Blackstone Griddle

1. Preheat the Blackstone griddle to medium-low to low heat (about 350° F).
2. Liberally coat the griddle with oil.
3. Add the fish, with the skin side of the salmon down if it has skin.
4. Cook for about 2 minutes per side for medium-rare, or until desired doneness. (Actual cook time will depend on the size and thickness of the salmon.)
5. Drizzle with freshly squeezed lemon juice and serve.

Pan-Frying Instructions

1. Heat a heavy skillet over medium heat and coat with oil.
2. Add the fish to the skillet, salmon skin side down.
3. Cook the fish for a total cooking time of about 4 to 5 minutes, flipping halfway through. Use an instant read thermometer to make sure that the center of the flesh has reached the desired doneness.

Nutritional Value (Amount per Serving):

Calories: 493; Fat: 19.66; Carb: 9.74; Protein: 70.55

Blackstone Cajun Catfish and Asparagus

Prep Time: 10 minutes   Cook Time: 10 minutes   Serves: 4

Ingredients:

- 4 catfish fillets
- 1 1/2 Tablespoons flour leave out if dong Keto/ low carb
- 1 1/2 Tablespoons Cajun seasoning
- cooking oil of choice or butter
- 1 pound asparagus bottom inch or two cut off
- Optional: spicy mayo, lemon wedges

Directions:

1. Pat the catfish fillets dry with paper towels. Sprinkle the flour on both sides and rub the flour to a thin, even layer. Season both sides with most of the Cajun seasoning (save some for the asparagus).
2. Preheat the griddle to medium heat for several minutes. Once hot add some cooking oil or butter and the seasoned catfish and asparagus. Sprinkle some Cajun seasoning on the asparagus as it hits the griddle.
3. Cook 8 to 10 minutes total, flipping the catfish halfway through and turning the asparagus a few times. The asparagus may be done before the catfish, if so remove before the fish.
4. Serve with spicy mayo and/or lemon wedges if desired.

Nutritional Value (Amount per Serving):

Calories: 327; Fat: 12.49; Carb: 26.27; Protein: 29.65

Teriyaki Shrimp Kabobs

Prep Time: 15 minutes   Cook Time: 10 minutes   Serves: 6

Ingredients:

- 3 pounds uncooked shrimp
- 2 cups pineapple chunks
- 1 teaspoon salt
- 1/2 teaspoon white pepper
- 2 tablespoons Maui Wowee Teriyaki Rub (optional)
- 3 tablespoons oil (avocado is best)
- Banchan Teriyaki Sauce

Directions:

1. Preheat your griddle over medium heat. Remove the shells and tails from the shrimp. Coat both sides of the shrimp with salt, white pepper, and the Maui Wowee Rub (if using).

2. Thread the shrimp onto your skewers along with the pineapple chunks.
3. Preheat your griddle over medium heat. Put a thin coat of oil down on the griddle surface.
4. Place the kabobs down and cook for 1-2 minutes per side, until the shrimp are pink and opaque throughout, or they reach a minimum internal temperature of 120°F.

Nutritional Value (Amount per Serving):

Calories: 367; Fat: 9.97; Carb: 19.94; Protein: 47.3

Blackstone Seared Scallops

Prep Time: 10 minutes   Cook Time: 8 minutes   Serves: 4

Ingredients:

- 2 pounds sea scallops
- 1 tablespoon sea salt
- 4 tablespoons avocado oil

Directions:

1. Preheat your griddle over medium high heat.
2. Dry the scallops on paper towels well. They can't be moist if you want a good crust on them.
3. Season the scallops with the salt on both sides.
4. Lay down the oil on the griddle surface and let preheat.
5. Place the scallops onto the oil, flat side down.
6. Let cook for 3-4 minutes, or until a golden brown crust has formed on the scallop's surface.
7. Flip, ensuring the scallop gets turned onto an oiled surface to make sure it won't stick.
8. Let cook another 3-4 minutes, or until the other side is also browned.
9. Remove from the griddle and serve hot.

Nutritional Value (Amount per Serving):

Calories: 376; Fat: 15.91; Carb: 12.27; Protein: 46.58

Spicy Broccoli Shrimp Stir Fry

Prep Time: 5 minutes   Cook Time: 15 minutes   Serves: 6 people

Ingredients:

Sauce
- 4 tablespoons soy sauce
- 4 tablespoons water
- 2 tablespoons mirin
- 1 teaspoon sesame oil

- 2 teaspoons minced garlic
- 2 teaspoons chili garlic sauce
- 1 teaspoon sriracha
- 2 tablespoons brown sugar

- 1/2 teaspoon ground ginger
- 1 1/2 tablespoons cornstarch
- 1 teaspoon canola oil

Stir Fry
- 2 pounds shrimp, peeled and deveined
- 4 cups broccoli florets
- 1 small onion, sliced

Directions:

1. Mix all the sauce ingredients together and stir well to combine.
2. Preheat the Blackstone to medium-high heat. Add a little oil to the griddle. Stir fry broccoli for 3-4 minutes and then cover with a dome.
3. Squirt a tablespoon of water under the dome and let steam.
4. Uncover, add some more oil to the griddle surface, and then add the shrimp.
5. Cook for 1 minute per side, and then pour the sauce over and cook until thickened, stirring constantly.

Nutritional Value (Amount per Serving):

Calories: 226; Fat: 5.98; Carb: 8.58; Protein: 32.83

Fish on the Blackstone

Prep Time: 5 minutes   Cook Time: 10 minutes   Serves: 1

Ingredients:

- 16 ounces boneless fish fillets
- 1 lemon, sliced into rounds
- 2 teaspoons flaky salt
- 1 teaspoon ground pepper
- 2 teaspoons lemon zest

- 1 tablespoon lemon juice
- 2 teaspoon garlic paste
- 4 teaspoons butter
- 4 tablespoons dry white wine
- 4 sprigs fresh thyme

Directions:

1. Prep your fish by feeling it to ensure there are no remaining bones. Season with salt and pepper.
2. Preheat your griddle to medium-low heat.
3. Mix together the lemon zest, lemon juice, and garlic paste.
4. Spread the lemon/garlic mixture over the top of each of the fish fillets.
5. Put down a small pat of butter on the griddle for each piece of fish you'll be cooking.
6. If your fish fillets have skin on one side, start them skin-side down on the griddle in the butter.
7. Place groups of two lemon slices down together on the griddle near each

other. This is what you're going to flip the fish ONTO. Put a sprig of thyme on top of the lemon slices.

8. After the fish cooks for 2-3 minutes, flip it onto the lemon slices and thyme. Cover them all with a cooking dome. Let it cook for 3-4 minutes, and then squirt some of the dry white wine under the dome and onto the lemons on the bottom to let the fish steam.
9. Remove from the griddle and serve immediately.
10. Slide the spatula right under the lemon and then carefully flip the whole lemon and filet onto the serving plate.

Nutritional Value (Amount per Serving):

Calories: 1122; Fat: 72.66; Carb: 16.26; Protein: 100.29

Blackstone Seared Bluefin Tuna with Togarashi

Prep Time: 5 minutes   Cook Time: 3 minutes   Serves: 1

Ingredients:

- 1 Bluefin Tuna Steak
- 1 tablespoon togarashi
- 1/2 teaspoon salt
- 1/4 teaspoon olive oil
- 1 teaspoon wasabi mayo
- 1 teaspoon sriracha mayo
- 3 tablespoons high-quality soy sauce

Directions:

1. Preheat your Blackstone over medium-high heat.
2. Pat dry your tuna steak and coat with the Togarashi and salt.
3. Drizzle the olive oil onto the surface of the preheated griddle. Place the tuna onto the oiled section.
4. Sear for about 30-45 seconds per side.
5. Remove and let rest for a minute before slicing thinly against the grain.
6. Drizzle with wasabi mayo and sriracha mayo, if desired. Serve with high quality soy sauce for a little dunking before eating.

Nutritional Value (Amount per Serving):

Calories: 560; Fat: 35.69; Carb: 6.15; Protein: 50.95

Sturgeon with Lemon Cream Sauce

Prep Time: 15 minutes   Cook Time: 15 minutes   Serves: 6

Ingredients:

Fish

- 3 pounds sturgeon fillets
- 3/4 teaspoon salt
- 3/4 teaspoon black pepper
- 1 1/2 teaspoon fresh thyme leaves

- 3 tablespoons salted butter
- 3 tablespoon olive oil
- 3 tablespoons water

Sauce

- 3 tablespoons olive oil
- 3 small shallots
- 3 garlic cloves, minced
- 1 lemon

- 1 tablespoon mushroom powder
- 2/3 cup cream
- 3 tablespoons salted butter
- 3 teaspoons chopped chives

Directions:

1. Preheat your griddle on medium high heat.
2. Sprinkle both sides of your fillets with salt, pepper and thyme.
3. Put 3 tablespoons butter and 3 tablespoons of your olive oil onto the grill. When the butter has melted, lay your fish down on top of it.
4. Let the fish cook for four minutes, and then flip it and cook for another four minutes on the other side.
5. Add the water in between your filets and cover with a domed lid. Let the fish cook for another 90 seconds, covered the whole time.
6. Use a small saute pan over medium heat, either on your griddle top or on your stove, and add the olive oil, shallots and garlic to the pan. Let cook for 4 minutes, stirring frequently.
7. Squeeze in the juice of half a lemon, add in the mushroom powder and your heavy cream. Let simmer for 30 seconds.
8. Remove from heat, and put in the pats of butter and whisk into the sauce until it melts.
9. Strain the sauce through a fine mesh strainer.
10. Serve the fish with a generous pour of sauce on top, and finish off with a squeeze of lemon and a sprinkle of chopped chives.

Nutritional Value (Amount per Serving):

Calories: 904; Fat: 67.18; Carb: 23.17; Protein: 53.22

Chapter 6: Poultry

Blackstone Chicken and Pea Pods

Prep Time: 20 minutes   Cook Time: 15 minutes   Serves: 8

Ingredients:

- 2 pounds chicken breasts
- 1 pound stringless sugar snap pea pods

Velveting Mixture

- 6 tablespoons water
- 6 tablespoons soy sauce
- 4 teaspoons cornstarch
- 4 teaspoons vegetable oil

Stir Fry Sauce

- 2 teaspoons sesame oil
- 6 tablespoons soy sauce
- 2 tablespoons black vinegar
- 1 teaspoon ginger
- 2 teaspoons chili garlic sauce
- 2 teaspoons honey
- 1 teaspoon gochujang
- 2 teaspoons garlic
- 4 tablespoons water
- 2 teaspoons cornstarch
- 2 teaspoons sesame seeds

Directions:

1. Slice the chicken into 1/4 inch thick strips across the grain.
2. Combine the water and soy sauce. Pour over the chicken breast, cover, and refrigerate for 20 minutes, stirring occasionally. By the end of the marinating time you want most of the liquid to be absorbed into the chicken.
3. Add the oil and cornstarch to the chicken mixture and stir until everything is evenly combined. Let sit another 15-20 minutes, covered in the fridge.
4. Preheat your Blackstone on high heat. Put down a thin layer of oil. Pre-cook your chicken in a single layer for about 20 seconds. Flip and cook the other side for an additional 20 seconds. It is okay if it isn't fully cooked at this point. Remove from the griddle into a clean bowl.
5. Scrape any bits off of the griddle and lay down some fresh oil and let it preheat again.
6. While the griddle is heating again, combine all of your stir-fry sauce ingredients in a bowl and whisk together.
7. Place the pea pods and chicken back on the preheated griddle and stir fry, stirring constantly with a large spatula, for 2 minutes. Pour the sauce over the chicken and pea pods and stir, coating all of the food, until the sauce has thickened and the chicken is cooked through.
8. Remove from the griddle and serve with rice and a sprinkle of sesame seeds.

Nutritional Value (Amount per Serving):

Calories: 341; Fat: 19.01; Carb: 14.15; Protein: 27.24

Blackstone Chicken Teriyaki

Prep Time: 20 minutes   Cook Time: 10 minutes   Serves: 6

Ingredients:

- 2 pound boneless skinless chicken breasts
- 2 tablespoons Maui Wowee Teriyaki Rub

Marinade

- 1/2 cup soy sauce
- 1/4 cup white vinegar
- 1/4 cup pineapple juice
- 1 teaspoon sriracha, optional

Teriyaki Sauce

- 1/4 cup water
- 1/4 cup pineapple juice
- 1/8 cup soy sauce
- 1 tablespoon brown sugar
- 1/4 teaspoon ground ginger
- 1/2 teaspoon minced garlic
- 1 tablespoon cornstarch
- 1/8 cup cold water

Directions:

1. Combine all of the marinade ingredients in a large container or gallon-sized freezer baggie. Cut the chicken into chunks and place it into the marinade. Let it marinate in the refrigerator for 2-4 hours.
2. While the chicken is having its soak, combine 1/4 cup water, pineapple juice, soy sauce, brown sugar, ground ginger, and minced garlic in a small saucepan. Heat over medium heat, stirring frequently, until it comes to a simmer.
3. Mix together the cold water and cornstarch with a whisk until there are no lumps, and then whisk into the simmering sauce. Cook until thickened, and set aside.
4. Preheat your griddle to medium-low heat. Drain off the marinade from the chicken, and then season with the Maui Wowee. Cook the chicken on the griddle surface, stirring and turning frequently, but letting it cook for a minute between stirrings to caramelize and brown a bit. Be careful not to overcook! It is done when there is no more pink, and when cut into bite-sized pieces this happens pretty quickly.
5. Serve with the homemade teriyaki sauce drizzled over alongside some steamed rice and a vegetable.

Nutritional Value (Amount per Serving):

Calories: 294; Fat: 8.83; Carb: 14.62; Protein: 36.4

Blackstone Chicken with Mushroom Gravy

Prep Time: 15 minutes   Cook Time: 20 minutes   Serves: 8

Ingredients:

Chicken
- 2 large boneless skinless chicken breasts
- 1 teaspoon avocado oil
- 1/4 teaspoon salt
- 1/4 teaspoon onion powder
- 1/4 teaspoon garlic powder
- 1/4 teaspoon black pepper

Mushrooms
- 1/2 cup chanterelle, (or other) mushrooms
- 1/4 teaspoon salt
- 1 tablespoon butter

Gravy
- 2 tablespoons butter
- 3 tablespoons flour
- 8 ounces chicken broth
- 1/4 teaspoon salt
- 1/4 teaspoon pepper
- 1 teaspoon powdered mushrooms
- 1/2 teaspoon chopped Italian parsley
- 1/2 teaspoon chopped chives

Directions:

1. Startup your flat top griddle and preheat it on medium-low heat.
2. Place a medium-sized cast iron on the griddle surface at the same time to preheat as well.
3. While you're waiting for your griddle to come up to temp, add your oil to your chicken breasts, and then season them with the dry ingredients.
4. After your griddle is heated, put your chicken breasts on the griddle and begin cooking them for six minutes per side. Chicken breasts are safe to eat after they have reached an internal temperature of at least 165 degrees Fahrenheit.
5. While the breasts are cooking, put your mushrooms, 1/4 teaspoon of salt, and 1 tablespoon of butter into the cast iron pan and sauté them.
6. Stir the mushrooms while they are cooking.
7. Keep cooking until the juices have been cooked out.
8. When the mushrooms have finished cooking, add the rest of your butter and the flour to the pan and cook it down for three minutes.
9. Next, add in your chicken broth and the rest of your dry ingredients as well as the parsley and chives.
10. Let the ingredients in the pan come to a simmer and then add the chicken breasts back into the pan and let cook for another three minutes or until the sauce starts to thicken.

11. Pull the pan from the grill and it is ready to serve.

Nutritional Value (Amount per Serving):

Calories: 171; Fat: 8.68; Carb: 2.8; Protein: 19.4

Blackstone Griddle Hibachi Chicken

Prep Time: 10 minutes   Cook Time: 20 minutes   Serves: 8

Ingredients:

For the vegetables:
- 2 medium zucchini sliced into spears
- 1/2 medium onion sliced
- 1 tablespoon butter
- 1 tablespoon avocado oil or your favorite cooking oil
- 1 teaspoon garlic powder
- 1-2 tablespoons soy sauce
- salt and pepper to taste

For the chicken:
- 11/2 pound boneless skinless chicken breast cut into cubes
- 2 tablespoons butter
- 1/4 cup soy sauce
- 2 tablespoons minced garlic
- 1 teaspoons minced ginger squeeze bottle ginger preferred
- 3 tablespoons honey
- 3 tablespoons brown sugar loosely packed
- yum yum sauce and/or siracha for serving

Directions:

1. Preheat griddle on low or medium low.
2. Start by preparing the fried rice recipe on the griddle.
3. While fried rice is cooking, in a medium bowl whisk together the sauce ingredients for the chicken including soy sauce, minced garlic, minced ginger, honey, and brown sugar. Set to the side.
4. When fried rice is almost done, move it to the cooler side of the griddle to make room to cook the other ingredients. Add about 1 tablespoon of butter and 1 tablespoon of avocado oil to the hotter zone of the griddle and spread it around a bit with your spatula. Add the zucchini and onions to the butter and oil and begin to sauté. Add garlic powder, soy sauce, salt, and pepper to the vegetables and mix to combine. Move zucchini and onions to the side of the griddle and continue to sauté until vegetables are tender.
5. Add about 1 tablespoon of avocado oil to the hotter zone on the griddle and spread it around a bit with your spatula. Add the cubed chicken breast to

the oiled griddle, making sure that the pieces are separated so that each is in contact with the griddle surface to get a nice sear.

6. Allow the chicken pieces to cook on the first side untouched for about 2 minutes. Then add about 2 tablespoons of butter to the chicken and toss to combine. Continue to sauté the chicken until almost all the way cooked through.

7. Add the hibachi sauce that you prepared earlier to the chicken on the griddle and toss to combine. Continue to sauté the chicken until it is cooked through and the sauce has slightly thickened. This will happen quickly (about 2 minutes).

8. Transfer all of the cooked Japanese steakhouse dishes (fried rice, teriyaki chicken, and zucchini and onions) to a large plate and serve immediately. Top with your favorite hibachi style sauces like yum yum sauce or siracha.

Nutritional Value (Amount per Serving):

Calories: 434; Fat: 13.86; Carb: 23.04; Protein: 55.51

Blackstone Chicken Quesadillas

Prep Time: 10 minutes   Cook Time: 10 minutes   Serves: 4

Ingredients:

- 1 lb Chicken Breast diced into 1-inch pieces
- 1 Tablespoon Vegetable Oil
- 2 Tablespoon Taco Seasoning
- 1/4 cup Salsa
- 1 1/2 cups Cheddar Cheese shredded
- 1 1/2 cups Monterey Jack Cheese shredded
- 4 Flour Tortillas burrito size

Directions:

1. Preheat the Blackstone Grill over medium high heat (approximately 400 degrees F). Spread the vegetable oil onto the grill.

2. Place the chicken onto the grill in an even layer. Season it with the taco seasoning. Sauté the chicken for 3-4 minutes per side until it's browned slightly. Then top the chicken with salsa and toss the chicken to thoroughly coat the chicken with the salsa. Continue to cook the chicken until it's cooked through (internal temperature of 165 degrees F) for approximately 3-4 more minutes.

3. Push the chicken to one side of the grill. Reduce the Blackstone temperature to medium.

4. Place the tortillas on the grill. Top each tortillas a small amount of each cheese, then layer the chicken on top and then add more cheese. Carefully

fold each the tortillas in half making a half moon shape.

5. Cook until one side of the tortilla is golden brown (1-2 minutes). Flip and then cook until the other side is golden brown as well (1-2 minutes). Watch them closely as they do brown quickly.

6. Remove the quesadillas onto a cutting board. Slice them and they are ready to serve and enjoy!

Nutritional Value (Amount per Serving):

Calories: 806; Fat: 43.34; Carb: 56.98; Protein: 46.23

Blackstone Griddle Cilantro Lime Chicken

Prep Time: 1 hours   Cook Time: 20 minutes   Serves: 4

Ingredients:

- 1/4 cup chopped fresh cilantro leaves
- 3 tablespoons extra virgin olive oil, divided
- 2 tablespoons freshly squeezed lime juice
- 1 tablespoon lime zest
- 2 teaspoons chili powder
- 1 teaspoon ground cumin
- 1 teaspoon kosher salt
- 1 teaspoon freshly ground black pepper
- 2 pounds boneless, skinless chicken breasts or tenderloins

Directions:

1. In a medium bowl, combine cilantro, olive oil, lime juice, lime zest, chili powder, cumin, salt and pepper.

2. In a gallon size Ziploc bag or large bowl, combine chicken and cilantro mixture; marinate for at least an hour to overnight, turning the bag occasionally. Remove the chicken from the marinade

3. Turn the Blackstone on high. Once it is heated, drizzle a little oil and butter onto the griddle.

4. Place the chicken on the Blackstone and let it cook about 4-5 minutes per side or until the chicken reaches 165 degrees internally.

5. Serve immediately with your favorite sides.

Nutritional Value (Amount per Serving):

Calories: 455; Fat: 18.47; Carb: 49.27; Protein: 22.32

Chicken Cutlets

Prep Time: 20 minutes   Cook Time: 10 minutes   Serves: 4

Ingredients:

- 4 boneless, skinless chicken breasts (about 2 pounds)
- 3 large eggs
- 1 cup all purpose flour
- 1 1/2 cup panko breadcrumbs
- 1 1/2 cup Italian style breadcrumbs
- 1/2 cup grated parmesan cheese
- Kosher salt and freshly ground black pepper
- Oil for frying

Directions:

1. If using full chicken breasts, slice in half horizontally and then pound them with a mallet until they are about 1/2 inch thick and relatively uniform. If using pre-cut chicken cutlets you can skip to the next step.
2. Season each piece of chicken with salt and pepper.
3. Add the breadcrumbs and cheese to a shallow bowl and mix together with your fingers.
4. In another shallow bowl, whisk 3 eggs with a pinch of salt and pepper and a tablespoon of water.
5. In a third shallow bowl, add the flour and season with salt and pepper. Mix to combine.
6. Set up your breading station. From left to right, you want the chicken on the far left, then the flour, then the egg, followed by the breadcrumbs and finally a plate or dish to hold the breaded chicken.
7. Take each piece of chicken and dredge in the flour, making sure to coat all sides. Tap off any excess.
8. Dip the floured chicken in the egg mixture. Coat it well and let any excess drip off.
9. Place the chicken in the breadcrumbs. Move it around so that it's completely coated and then transfer to the empty plate.
10. Preheat your Blackstone griddle to medium heat.
11. Pour a small pool of oil onto the cooking surface (enough that the entire chicken breast is in the oil) and place the chicken directly on it.
12. Cook until golden brown on each side (about 6 to 8 minutes total), then remove and place on a rack or paper towels to absorb excess oil.
13. Sprinkle with Kosher salt while still warm and serve immediately.

Nutritional Value (Amount per Serving):

Calories: 710; Fat: 28.74; Carb: 79.25; Protein: 32.53

Teriyaki Chicken Thighs

Prep Time: 3 minutes   Cook Time: 12 minutes   Serves: 5

Ingredients:

- 1/4 cup paleo teriyaki sauce
- 5 skinless boneless chicken thighs

Directions:

1. Trim any excess fat from the chicken thighs.
2. In a large baggie or bowl add the teriyaki sauce and chicken thighs. Coat evenly.
3. Let the chicken thighs marinate for 30 minutes at room temperature.
4. Preheat Blackstone over medium high heat. Once hot, add the boneless skinless teriyaki chicken thighs.
5. Cook for 6-8 minutes on each side until the chicken thighs reach an internal temperature of 165F.
6. Remove chicken thighs from the flat top grill. Wait 5 minutes before eating.

Nutritional Value (Amount per Serving):

Calories: 285; Fat: 5.95; Carb: 2.24; Protein: 51.88

Blackstone Buffalo Chicken Loaded Potatoes

Prep Time: 15 minutes   Cook Time: 20 minutes   Serves: 6

Ingredients:

- 1 1/2 pounds red potatoes
- 1 1/2 pounds boneless, skinless chicken thighs or breasts
- 6 slices bacon
- cooking oil of choice
- kosher salt, pepper
- 1 packet dry ranch seasoning
- 1/2 cup buffalo wing sauce
- 2 cups shredded cheese
- Optional toppings: green onions, sour cream, ranch dressing

Directions:

1. Cut the potatoes and chicken into bite size pieces and place them separated on a tray. Place all the other ingredients on the tray, keep everything separated from the raw chicken.
2. Carry the tray with the ingredients out to the Blackstone and preheat the griddle to medium heat for several minutes.
3. Place the bacon slices on the griddle and cook 3 to 4 minutes per side or until the bacon is cooked. Remove the bacon from the griddle, let it cool, and crumble into smaller pieces, set aside.
4. Add some cooking oil to the griddle along with the diced potatoes, kosher

salt, and pepper. Cook the potatoes for 9 to 11 minutes turning and flipping a few times with your hibachi spatulas.

5. Add more cooking oil and the chicken to the griddle with the potatoes along with more kosher salt and pepper. Cook 9 to 11 minutes stirring and flipping a few times with the potatoes.

6. Once the chicken is cooked and the potatoes are cooked how you prefer add the dry ranch seasoning and wing sauce, cook a minute or two combining everything together with the hibachi spatulas.

7. Spread the chicken and potatoes in an even layer on the griddle. Sprinkle the cheese and bacon crumbles over top and wait for the cheese to melt, you can turn the griddle off while waiting for the cheese to melt.

8. Sprinkle with green onions, sour cream, and or ranch dressing if desired.

Nutritional Value (Amount per Serving):

Calories: 614; Fat: 31.33; Carb: 55.47; Protein: 27.59

Chapter 7: Beef & Pork and Lamb

Blackstone Beef and Broccoli

Prep Time: 5 minutes   Cook Time: 10 minutes   Serves: 6

Ingredients:

- 2 pounds thinly sliced steak
- 3 cups broccoli florets

Steak Seasoning
- 1 teaspoon salt
- 1/2 teaspoon granulated garlic
- 1/2 teaspoon Chinese Five Spice

Sauce
- 1/2 cup water
- 1/4 cup soy sauce
- 2 tablespoons brown sugar
- 2 tablespoons corn starch
- 1 tablespoon mirin

- 3 tablespoons avocado oil

- 1/4 teaspoon onion powder
- 1/4 teaspoon pepper

- 1 tablespoon rice vinegar
- 1 teaspoon minced garlic
- 1 teaspoon Johnny's Au Jus Powder (optional)
- 1/4 teaspoon minced ginger

Directions:

1. Preheat your griddle over high heat.
2. While the griddle preheats, mix together your steak seasoning and evenly coat all of the thinly sliced steak.
3. In a small bowl, whisk together the sauce ingredients until there are no more lumps from the corn starch.
4. Add the avocado oil to the preheated griddle. Put the broccoli down and stir fry for 2-3 minutes. Pile it up and add some water to the middle before covering with a domed lid.
5. Add the beef to the griddle and let it brown on both sides. Flip and chop it as it cooks into bite-sized pieces.
6. Combine the broccoli and the beef and drizzle the sauce over the top.
7. Stir and flip continuously for 2-3 minutes, until the sauce is cooked and thickened and is coating the broccoli and beef.
8. Remove from the griddle and serve hot.

Nutritional Value (Amount per Serving):

Calories: 598; Fat: 50.02; Carb: 10.98; Protein: 26.79

Blackstone Flank Steak

Prep Time: 10 minutes   Cook Time: 15 minutes   Serves: 4

Ingredients:

- 2 pound flank steak

- 2 teaspoons salt

- 1 teaspoon pepper

Chimichurri
- 1 shallot, chopped
- 4 cloves garlic, chopped
- 1/2 cup red wine vinegar
- 1 teaspoon kosher salt

- 2 tablespoons butter

- 1/4 cup chopped flat-leaf parsley
- 1/2 cup chopped cilantro
- 2 tablespoons chopped oregano
- ¾ cup extra-virgin olive oil

Directions:

1. Preheat your Blackstone griddle to medium-high heat.
2. Pat your steak dry with paper towels and season on both sides with salt and pepper.
3. Put down on the griddle and press down gently to ensure an even sear across the entire surface.
4. Flip once the first side gets a good sear and continue to sear the other side until the internal temperature reaches about 120-125°F. Remove from the griddle and let the steak rest, tented, for 10-15 minutes.
5. Slice against the grain into thin slices. Serve hot, with chimichurri on top or for dipping.

Nutritional Value (Amount per Serving):

Calories: 557; Fat: 34.91; Carb: 7.94; Protein: 50.35

Blackstone Teriyaki Meatballs

Prep Time: 10 minutes   Cook Time: 20 minutes   Serves: 4

Ingredients:

- 1 pound ground pork
- 3 tablespoons crushed pineapple
- 1/2 cup panko bread crumbs
- 1 tablespoon milk
- 1 egg
- 2 teaspoons Togarashi (or another good Asian rub)
- 2 tablespoons oil
- 1/4 cup pineapple juice
- 1 cup Bachan's Japanese BBQ Sauce
- 1 tablespoon sweet and sour

Directions:

1. Mix together the ground pork, drained crushed pineapple, panko, milk, egg, and Togarashi in a bowl until they are well combined.
2. Form into small 1"-1 1/2" meatballs.
3. Preheat your griddle over medium heat.
4. Lay down the oil on the griddle and put the meatballs on.

5. Brown on all sides, turning frequently.
6. Mix together the pineapple juice with 1/4 cup of your Bachan's. Gather the meatballs all together on the griddle in a bunch, pour this mixture over the top, and immediately cover with a large dome.
7. Using the dome, move the meatballs around a bit on the griddle so they get coated with the sauce. This will also assure that your meatballs are fully cooked.
8. Remove from the griddle and serve over steamed rice with the extra Bachan's and Sweet and Sour drizzled over the top.

Nutritional Value (Amount per Serving):

Calories: 483; Fat: 33.29; Carb: 11.84; Protein: 33.22

Smoked Corned Beef Hash on the Griddle

Prep Time: 10 minutes   Cook Time: 20 minutes   Serves: 6

Ingredients:

- 4 cups diced potatoes (frozen is fine)
- 3 tablespoons oil
- 1/4 teaspoon salt
- 1/2 teaspoon onion powder
- 1/2 teaspoon paprika
- 1/4 teaspoon granulated garlic
- 1/4 teaspoon cracked black pepper
- 4 tablespoons butter
- 2/3 cup chopped onion
- 2/3 cup chopped bell pepper
- 2 cups cubed corned beef
- 4 poached eggs
- 1 tablespoon chopped fresh parsley

Directions:

1. Preheat your gas griddle (or cast iron pan on the stovetop) over medium-high heat. Let it get nice and hot! A big outdoor gas griddle will take ALL of 10 minutes to fully preheat. Don't rush it!
2. Toss the diced potatoes in the oil and seasonings.
3. Pour the potatoes out onto a lightly oiled griddle, place a tablespoon of butter on the top of the potatoes, cover with a dome, and let cook for 3-5 minutes.
4. Check the potatoes and if they are browned on the bottom flip. If not, continue cooking until they are lightly browned.
5. On the other part of the griddle (or in another cast iron pan), brush a light coating of oil on it and then lay down the onion and bell pepper. Add some more butter too for good measure. Cook the onions and bell peppers, stirring frequently, until they are softened and starting to get lightly browned.
6. During the last few minutes of cooking the potatoes, put down some more

butter and the corned beef near the potatoes. Heat until everything is warmed through, flipping as needed.

7. Once the potatoes are fully cooked and browned, mix together the onions and corned beef with the potatoes. Turn the griddle down to low, cover, and cook the eggs. You can fry or poach them, depending on what you prefer.
8. Sprinkle some parsley on top before serving. Salt to taste. How much total you'll need depends on your personal preferences, what kind of potatoes you use, and how salty the corned beef is.

Nutritional Value (Amount per Serving):

Calories: 401; Fat: 25.37; Carb: 20.25; Protein: 23.92

Blackstone Seattle Cheesesteak

Prep Time: 10 minutes   Cook Time: 15 minutes   Serves: 8

Ingredients:

- 1 teaspoon salt, divided
- 1/2 teaspoon black pepper, divided
- 1 teaspoon Old Bay seasoning, divided
- 2 bell peppers, sliced
- 1 medium white or yellow onion, sliced
- 1 teaspoon olive oil
- 1/2 cup mayonnaise
- 1/4 shredded parmesan cheese
- 4 fresh hoagie rolls
- 8 tablespoons butter, divided
- 1 pound Dungeness crab meat
- 4 ounces aged cheddar cheese

Directions:

1. Preheat your griddle over medium heat.
2. Place your vegetables into a bowl and drizzle in the olive oil. Season the oiled vegetables with 1/2 teaspoon salt, 1/4 teaspoon pepper, and 1/2 teaspoon Old Bay seasoning.
3. In a small bowl mix the mayonnaise, parmesan cheese, and 1/4 teaspoon black pepper. Set aside.
4. Sauté the vegetables on the griddle, stirring occasionally.
5. While the vegetables sauté, split your hoagie buns down the middle. Butter the inside with 1 tablespoon of butter (approximately) per hoagie roll, and place on the griddle top to toast. After they are toasted and golden brown, pull them from the griddle and set aside.

6. When your vegetables have been on the grill for about five minutes, add your butter to another part of the griddle and lay all of your crab meat on top.
7. Spread the crab out flat onto the griddle, so that it is about 1-inch thick. Sprinkle the crab with 1/2 teaspoon salt.
8. Separate the crab meat into four distinct piles of about 4 ounces each, and the general length and with of the hoagie roll. 6" is ideal length for most rolls. Spoon out two tablespoons of the mayonnaise and parmesan mix onto each pile.
9. Place a nice slice of the cheddar cheese on top of the mayo/parmesan mix, and cover the crab and cheese until the cheddar cheese has melted.
10. Add a layer of peppers and onion to the bottom of your hoagie rolls.
11. Place the crab on top of your vegetables on the rolls.
12. Sprinkle the rest of your Old Bay on top of the melted cheese. Serve hot.

Nutritional Value (Amount per Serving):

Calories: 436; Fat: 21.61; Carb: 36.08; Protein: 27.87

Sous Vide London Broil

Prep Time: 10 hours   Cook Time: 10 minutes   Serves: 6

Ingredients:

- 3-pound London Broil
- 3 tablespoons olive oil
- 1 teaspoon salt
- 1/2 teaspoon pepper

Directions:

1. Dry the London Broil and rub with olive oil. Season with salt and pepper and carefully place it into the vacuum seal bag and seal.
2. Preheat the sous vide to 130°F. Place the London Broil in the Sous Vide water bath and cook for 8-12 hours.
3. Remove from the water bath, take out of the package, and put it into a hot cast-iron pan to sear on both sides.
4. Rest for 10-15 minutes before slicing.

Nutritional Value (Amount per Serving):

Calories: 524; Fat: 27.17; Carb: 0.35; Protein: 69.63

Filet Mignon with Lobster

Prep Time: 10 minutes   Cook Time: 10 minutes   Serves: 1

Ingredients:

- 1 6-ounce filet mignon
- 1 4-ounce lobster tail

- 1/4 teaspoon salt
- 1/8 teaspoon pepper
- 1/8 teaspoon garlic powder
- 1 tablespoon butter
- 1/2 teaspoon Old Bay seasoning

Directions:

1. Preheat your griddle on medium-high heat according to factory instructions.
2. Remove the meat from the lobster tail.
3. Mix your salt, pepper, and garlic powder together and sprinkle it on both sides of your steak and lobster tail. Sprinkle the Old Bay seasoning onto both sides of the lobster tail.
4. Put 1/2 of the butter onto the griddle top and put your steak on top of it. Let your steak cook for 3 minutes and then flip it. Cook for another three minutes and then check the temperature. Pull the steak from the grill when the internal temperature reaches 125 degrees F and let it rest for five minutes.
5. While your steak is resting, add the rest of your butter to the grill top and put the lobster tail on top of it. Flip the lobster after 2 minutes and cook for another 2 minutes. Place a dome on top if you have one available.
6. Pull the lobster from the grill and place it on top of your steak and serve.

Nutritional Value (Amount per Serving):

Calories: 420; Fat: 20.33; Carb: 1.15; Protein: 57.61

Snake River Farms American Wagyu Manhattan Filet

Prep Time: 10-15 minutes   Cook Time: 15 minutes   Serves: 1 Steak

Ingredients:

- 1 6-ounce Manhattan Filet
- salt
- pepper
- butter
- garlic clove

Directions:

1. Preheat your Blackstone over low heat. If using a cast-iron pan on the stovetop, you'll want to increase the heat to medium.
2. Let the steak rest for 10-15 minutes before cooking.
3. Place a teaspoon of butter onto the griddle and then put the steak on top. Don't touch it for several minutes, 4-5 is typical, or however long it takes for a crust to develop. Let the garlic cook next to the steak, and rub it over the steak periodically.
4. Sprinkle salt on the steak periodically as you are cooking it.
5. Lift the steak from the griddle, put down some more butter, and then flip it onto the uncooked side. Let that side develop a crust too.

6. Continue to put down additional butter, as needed, and cook each side of the steak until a dark brown crust has developed. Continue cooking until the internal temperature reaches your desired level of doneness. We cook ours to about 120° before the rest.
7. Remove from the griddle and let rest for 10 minutes, tented in foil, before cutting.

Nutritional Value (Amount per Serving):

Calories: 393; Fat: 23.68; Carb: 5.32; Protein: 40.57

Reverse Seared T-Bone Steak

Prep Time: 10 minutes   Cook Time: 2 minutes   Serves: 6

Ingredients:

- 2 pounds T-bone steak
- salt & pepper

Directions:

1. Preheat your pellet grill or smoker to 200°F. Place the steak on and let it cook until they reach 115°F internal temperature.
2. Remove from the grill and liberally salt and pepper the steaks. Preheat a gas griddle or cast iron pan over medium-high heat, and lay down a bit of oil in the pan or on the griddle.
3. Place the steak on and sear for 1-2 minutes on each side.
4. Let rest, covered, for 5 minutes before cutting.

Nutritional Value (Amount per Serving):

Calories: 348; Fat: 23.96; Carb: 0.74; Protein: 30.35

Reverse-Seared Flat Iron Steak

Prep Time: 10 minutes   Cook Time: 2 minuts   Serves: 6

Ingredients:

- 6 flat iron steaks
- salt & pepper

Directions:

1. Preheat your pellet grill or smoker to 200°F. Place the steaks on and let them cook until they reach 115°F internal temperature.
2. Remove from the grill and liberally salt and pepper the steaks. Preheat a gas griddle or cast iron pan over medium-high heat, and lay down a bit of oil in the pan or on the griddle.
3. Place the steaks on, and sear for 1-2 minutes on each side.
4. Let rest, covered, for 5 minutes before cutting.

Nutritional Value (Amount per Serving):

Calories: 443; Fat: 26.32; Carb: 0.74; Protein: 47.59

Blackstone Sirloin Cap Steak

Prep Time: 5 minutes   Cook Time: 10 minutes   Serves: 6

Ingredients:

- Top Sirloin Cap Steak
- salt
- pepper
- butter

Directions:

Direct Sear Method

1. Preheat your Blackstone to medium heat. Season your steak with salt and pepper, and place on the grill.
2. Leave it alone for several minutes! You want time for that crust to develop. But dollop some butter near it during the cook.
3. Turn the steak and let it cook on the other side until a crust develops there too.
4. More butter, more turning, more sizzle, until the steak is at your desired temperature. Use a meat thermometer for the best results until you get a good feel for things! You want to hit about 125°F when you pull it for a medium-rare steak when it is sliced.

Reverse Sear Method

1. Season your meat and place it on a smoker at 180°-200°F. Let the steak reverse sear for about an hour, or until the internal temperature reaches about 120°F.
2. Remove from the pellet grill or smoker, and place onto a preheated flat top griddle at medium-high to high heat. Let sear for 2-3 minutes per side to develop a crust.

Nutritional Value (Amount per Serving):

Calories: 286; Fat: 21.45; Carb: 0.71; Protein: 21.25

Blackstone Beef Kabob

Prep Time: 20 minutes   Cook Time: 10 minutes   Serves: 4

Ingredients:

For the marinade:

- 1/4 cup olive oil
- 2 tablespoons soy sauce

- 2 tablespoons Worcestershire sauce
- 2 tablespoons balsamic vinegar
- 2 cloves garlic, minced
- 1 teaspoon Dijon mustard
- 1 teaspoon herbs, (such as thyme, rosemary, or oregano)
- 1 teaspoon kosher salt
- 1/2 teaspoon black pepper

For the kebabs:
- 1 1/2 pounds beef steak, (such as sirloin, ribeye, or tenderloin), cut into 1-inch cubes
- 1 large red bell pepper, cut into chunks
- 1 large green bell pepper, cut into chunks
- 1 large yellow bell pepper, cut into chunks
- 1 large red onion, diced
- Optional: Cherry tomatoes, mushrooms, zucchini, or any other vegetables you prefer

Directions:

1. Begin by preparing the marinade. Combine the olive oil, soy sauce, Worcestershire sauce, balsamic vinegar, minced garlic, Dijon mustard, dried herbs, salt, and pepper in a bowl. Whisk the ingredients together until well combined, creating a flavorful marinade for the steak.
2. Place the beef steak cubes in a resealable plastic bag or a shallow dish. Pour the marinade over the steak, ensuring all the pieces are well coated.
3. Seal the bag or cover the dish, and refrigerate for at least 1 hour or overnight. This marinating process allows the flavors to meld and the steak to become tender and infused with the delicious marinade.
4. Preheat your Blackstone griddle to medium-high heat, ensuring it reaches the desired temperature before grilling the kebabs. Thread the marinated beef steak cubes onto the skewers, alternating with the bell peppers, onions, and any other vegetables you choose to include. This arrangement provides a beautiful combination of colors and flavors on each kebab.
5. Lightly oil the griddle surface to prevent sticking. Carefully place the assembled kebabs on the hot griddle, ensuring enough space between them for cooking.
6. Grill the kebabs for approximately 8-10 minutes, turning them occasionally to ensure even cooking on all sides. The cooking time may vary depending on the thickness of the steak cubes and your preferred level of doneness. Aim for medium-rare to medium for juicy and tender results, adjusting the cooking time accordingly.
7. Once the steak is cooked to your desired level, remove the kebabs from the griddle and allow them to rest for a few minutes. This resting period allows the juices to redistribute, ensuring optimal tenderness and flavor.

Nutritional Value (Amount per Serving):

Calories: 433; Fat: 24.55; Carb: 13.97; Protein: 37.94

Beef Stroganoff

Prep Time: 20 minutes   Cook Time: 20 minutes   Serves: 6

Ingredients:

- 1 yellow onion, sliced
- 8 ounces brown mushrooms, quartered
- 1 large portobello mushroom, sliced
- 1 pound shaved steak
- 1 (16-ounce) bag egg noodles, cooked
- 1 (8-ounce) tub sour cream (plus additional for dolloping)
- 3 tablespoons Better Than Bouillon beef paste
- 1/2 cup water
- 1 bunch green onions, sliced
- Salt and pepper, to taste
- Vegetable oil, for the griddle

Directions:

1. Preheat a griddle or large flat cooking surface to medium heat. Drizzle some vegetable oil onto the griddle.
2. Add the onions, brown mushrooms, and sliced Portobello mushroom to the griddle. Season with salt and pepper and cook for about 5 minutes until the mushrooms are tender and the onions are translucent.
3. Push the mushrooms and onions to one side of the griddle and add the shaved steak to the other side. Season the steak with salt and pepper and cook for about 3 minutes until it is well done.
4. Add the cooked egg noodles to the griddle and stir with spatulas until the steak, mushrooms, and noodles are evenly mixed.
5. In a small bowl, combine the Better Than Bouillon beef paste with 1/2 cup of water to create a slurry.
6. Pour the slurry, along with the sour cream, over the noodles. Stir with spatulas for about 2 minutes until a creamy sauce is formed, coating the meat and noodles.
7. Use spatulas to transfer the stroganoff onto a large serving platter.
8. Dollop additional sour cream on top of the stroganoff.
9. Sprinkle with black pepper and sliced green onions for garnish. Serve immediately.

Nutritional Value (Amount per Serving):

Calories: 331; Fat: 19.08; Carb: 12.74; Protein: 28.66

Corned Beef Reuben

Prep Time: 2 minutes   Cook Time: 5 minutes   Serves: 1

Ingredients:

- Bread, Rye, Sliced 2 each
- Butter, Softened 1 tablespoon
- Cheese, Swiss, Slices 2 each
- Corned Beef, Sliced 4 ounces
- Sauerkraut, Drained 1/2 cup
- Thousand Island Dressing. 1 tablespoon

Directions:

1. Gather the ingredients before you start.
2. Heat the Blackstone griddle. For a Blackstone griddle gas grill, preheat on medium. If using an electric Blackstone, preheat the flat top griddle to 400°F.
3. While the Blackstone griddle is heating up, lightly butter one side of each piece of the rye bread. Place two slices of Swiss cheese on top of one side of the non-butter rye bread slice. When the flat top griddle is hot, place both slices of the bread on the Blackstone so the buttered side is down.
4. In another spot on the griddle, spread out the sliced pieces of corned beef.
5. On the piece of rye bread without the Swiss cheese, top with the sauerkraut that has been rinsed and drained, so it is not dripping. The last thing you want is soggy bread.
6. Toss the sliced corned beef around on the hot griddle to evenly cook and heat up.
7. Assemble the Blackstone Reuben sandwich by placing the warmed corned beef slices on top of the sauerkraut piece of bread and flip the sandwich on top of the other half. Griddle grilling the corned beef Rueben sandwich will take about 3 to 5 minutes. Serve the Corned Beef Rueben sandwiches warm with Thousand Island dressing and your favorite sides.

Nutritional Value (Amount per Serving):

Calories: 607; Fat: 33.2; Carb: 33.81; Protein: 43.83

Pulled Pork Burritos (Wet)

Prep Time: 5 minutes   Cook Time: 5 minutes   Serves: 6

Ingredients:

- Tortillas, Soft Taco Shells, large 1 each
- Pulled Pork, Shredded 1/2 cup
- Enchilada Sauce, Red 1/2 cup
- Cheese, Shredded, Colby Jack 1 cup

Directions:

1. Gather all of the ingredients to make your pulled pork wet burrito recipe.
2. Heat the pulled pork to warm it up a little bit.
3. Place the soft shell tortilla on a plate or serving pan.
4. Place the warm pulled pork in the center of the soft tortilla shell.
5. To Fold Pulled Pork Burritos, fold opposite sides of the soft shell into the center. Fold the ends in and roll over so everything is tucked under the burrito.
6. After you have folded your burrito and flipped it over on your plate, pour about the red enchilada sauce over top the burrito.
7. Sprinkle about 1 cup of the shredded cheese over the sauce. Melt the cheese in the microwave or under a broiler.
8. Top the wet burrito with your desired toppings such as shredded lettuce, diced tomatoes or onions, sliced olives, a dollop of sour cream or avocado guacamole.
9. Serve piping hot with your favorite beverage.

Nutritional Value (Amount per Serving):

Calories: 143; Fat: 9.65; Carb: 3.37; Protein: 10.54

Steak and Eggs

Prep Time: 5 minutes   Cook Time: 15 minutes   Serves: 1

Ingredients:

- Steak 8 ounces
- Olive Oil 1 teaspoon
- Salt 1/4 teaspoon
- Pepper 1/8 teaspoon
- Herb Garlic Butter. 2 teaspoons
- Egg 1 each

Directions:

1. Prepare the herb garlic butter up ahead of time, if needed, so that it is ready to go when needed.
2. Remove the steak from the refrigerator 1 hour before you plan on cooking it and just leave on the countertop to come to room temperature.
3. Preheat the Blackstone flat top griddle to medium heat or if using the Blackstone Electric Griddle set the dial to 350°F.
4. Season the steak with your favorite steak seasoning, such as Lawry's Seasoned Salt and Morton Natures Seasonings.
5. Once the Blackstone griddle is hot, lightly oil the flat top griddle with some olive oil and a griddle spatula.
6. Place the steak on the preheated griddle and let cook 3 to 4 minutes without moving to let the steak get a good deep golden-brown color on it.
7. Use a griddle spatula and flip the steak over.

8. Add a dollop of garlic butter to the top center of the griddle steak. Let the garlic butter melt into the steak as it continues to cook. If desired, you can add more then one pat of the compound butter. The basil garlic butter will melt and create a butter sauce around the steak will it cooks.

9. Cook the Blackstone griddle steak to your desired doneness. Use a digital thermometer to check the temperature or do the touch test. Cooking times will vary depending on the griddle temperature, the thickness and size of your steak, the temperature of the steak, and the surrounding air temperature.

10. Let the butter steak rest for 5 minutes.

11. Make your fried eggs to go on the top of the steak. Crack an egg into a bowl or just crack it right onto the hot flat top griddle. Make sure the griddle is on medium heat and there is a thin layer of olive oil or butter.

12. You may also choose to cook the fried egg into the leftover steak drippings. Add one egg onto the hot griddle. Season with your favorite seasonings. Do not move while it is cooking. If you want the whites or yolks set on the egg, then cover with a dome lid to help in the cooking process.

13. When your egg is cooked to the desired doneness, remove from the Blackstone griddle and place on top of the resting steak.

14. Serve hot.

Nutritional Value (Amount per Serving):

Calories: 663; Fat: 40.96; Carb: 1.58; Protein: 72.24

Garlic Butter Steaks

Prep Time: 5 minutes   Cook Time: 10 minutes   Serves: 1

Ingredients:

- Steak 8 ounces
- Olive Oil 1 teaspoon
- Salt 1/4 teaspoon
- Pepper 1/8 teaspoon
- Herb Garlic Butter. 2 teaspoons

Directions:

1. Make the herb garlic butter up ahead of time so that it is ready to go when needed.

2. Remove the steak from the refrigerator 2 hours before you plan on cooking it and just leave on the countertop to come to room temperature.

3. Preheat the Blackstone griddle to medium heat or if using the Blackstone E-Series Griddle set the dial to 350°F.

4. Next, season the steak with your favorite steak seasoning.

5. Once the Blackstone griddle has come to temp, lightly oil the flat top

griddle with some olive oil.

6. Place the steak on the preheated griddle and let cook 4 to 5 minutes without moving to let the meat get a good deep golden-brown color on it.
7. Use a griddle spatula and flip the seared steak over.
8. Add the dollop of herb garlic butter to the top center of the cooking steak. Let the garlic butter melt into the steak as it cooks. If desired, you can add more than one pat of the garlic compound butter. The basil garlic butter will melt and create a butter sauce that the steak will cook in.
9. Cook the griddle steak to your desired doneness. Use a digital meat thermometer to check the temperature or do the touch test. Cooking times will vary depending on the griddle temperature, the thickness and size of the steak, the temperature of the steak, and the surrounding air temperature.
10. Let the butter steak rest for 5 minutes before serving.

Nutritional Value (Amount per Serving):

Calories: 534; Fat: 31.32; Carb: 0.56; Protein: 63.28

Cheese & Bacon Hasselback Potatoes

Prep Time: 2 minutes   Cook Time: 50 minutes   Serves: 2

Ingredients:

- Potatoes, Russet 2 each
- Butter, Softened 2 tablespoons
- Simple Three, Seasoning. 1 teaspoon
- Bacon Bits 2 tablespoons
- Cheese, Shredded. 1/4 cup

Directions:

1. Gather all the ingredients to make your Hasselback Potato Recipe.
2. Wash your potatoes well! Use a scrub brush to get all the dirt off if needed. The last thing you want is to bite into a sandy potato.
3. Dry completely.
4. With a sharp knife, make your slices into the potato making sure NOT to cut all the way through. Leave a little bit on the bottom to help keep the potato together. If you want crispier pieces of potatoes, cut very thin slices. But if you want softer pieces then cut your slices a little thicker.
5. Next, take one tablespoon of soft butter and spread all over your potato.
6. Sprinkle some of the Northern Spice Co. - Simply Three seasoning onto the outside of the potato.
7. Wrap the buttered potato in a piece of foil.
8. Preheat your Blackstone griddle to the lowest setting. It is very important

to cook these potatoes low and slow.

9. Once the griddle is preheated, then place the foil wrapped Hasselback Potatoes onto the griddle and cover with a dome lid.

10. Turn the potatoes about every 10-15 minutes with a pair of tongs.

11. After about 45 minutes, open the foil and check the potatoes for doneness by testing the center. If they are done, carefully separate or fan the potato slices.

12. Sprinkle with bacon bits and a generous amount of shredded cheese.

13. Leave the cheesy Hasselback potatoes unwrapped but still in the foil.

14. Place back on the griddle under the dome lid and let cook until the cheese is thoroughly melted.

15. Serve hot. Add your favorite topping such as a drizzle of ranch dressing, a dollop of sour cream along with a sprinkle of chives.

Nutritional Value (Amount per Serving):

Calories: 467; Fat: 15.1; Carb: 69.99; Protein: 15.04

Blackstone Steak Fajitas

Prep Time: 30 minutes   Cook Time: 10 minutes   Serves: 12

Ingredients:

- 6 pounds steak
- 2 teaspoons salt
- 1/2 teaspoon pepper
- 2 tablespoons The Spice Guy Fajita seasoning**, divided
- 1 small can El Pato Jalapeno Salsa
- 3 bell peppers, multi-colored
- 1 large onion
- 3 tablespoons avocado oil
- tortillas, of your choice

Directions:

1. Slice your steak into thin strips again the grain. Season with salt, pepper, and 1 1/2 tablespoons of the Fajita seasoning. Place it in a container or plastic baggie. Add in the El Pato Jalapeno Salsa and let sit for 30 minutes.

2. While your steak is sitting, slice your vegetables and season with the remaining Fajita seasoning.

3. Preheat your Blackstone griddle over high heat for 10-15 minutes. Lay down your oil and spread it out evenly before putting down your meat on one side of the griddle and veggies on the other.

4. Cook the steak, flipping occasionally until it is at your desired level of doneness. Remove the vegetables from the griddle when they are still

tender-crisp.

5. Heat your tortillas on the griddle briefly before serving with all of your favorite fajita toppings.

Nutritional Value (Amount per Serving):

Calories: 517; Fat: 26.78; Carb: 5.72; Protein: 64

Blackstone Skirt Steak Street Tacos

Prep Time: 10 minutes   Cook Time: 10 minutes   Serves: 8

Ingredients:

- 4 pounds beef skirt steak
- 2 limes, juiced
- 1 teaspoon salt
- 1/2 teaspoon pepper
- 1/2 teaspoon garlic powder
- 1 tablespoon chile lime rub from Spiceology
- corn tortillas
- 1 small white onion, finely diced
- 1 bunch cilantro, chopped
- hot sauce of your choosing

Directions:

1. Take the steak and evenly distribute all of the salt, pepper, garlic powder, and chile-lime rub. Let it sit in the fridge uncovered and seasoned for about an hour. (You can skip this step if you are short on time.)
2. While the steak is waiting, chop all of your veggies.
3. Preheat your Blackstone Gas Griddle over medium heat for 10-15 minutes.
4. Lay down a thin layer of oil and warm all of your tortillas on both sides on the griddle. Wrap in foil tightly so they stay nice and warm.
5. Cut the steak across the grain into thin strips, and then cut across all of the strips to dice the uncooked steak into bite-sized pieces.
6. Lay down a little more oil and throw the steak down in a thin layer on the hot griddle.
7. Let the steak sizzle and cook for a couple of minutes until it starts getting a light crust on the bottom.
8. Flip all the steak using a large spatula onto the other side and stir it up a bit. Squeeze your lime juice onto the steak and stir it around, and then remove it promptly from the griddle.
9. Serve in your hot tortillas with your garnish and enjoy!

Nutritional Value (Amount per Serving):

Calories: 565; Fat: 28.69; Carb: 12.93; Protein: 60.82

Blackstone Philly Cheesesteaks

Prep Time: 5 minutes   Cook Time: 10 minutes   Serves: 6

Ingredients:

- 3 pounds thinly sliced ribeye
- 1 tablespoon oil
- salt
- pepper
- provolone or cheese whiz
- buns
- butter
- peppers and onions (optional)

Directions:

1. Preheat your gas griddle over medium heat until it is preheated. Butter your buns and give them a quick toast.
2. On one half of the griddle, put down some butter and the onions and peppers if you are going that direction, and on the other half throw down some oil. Let it preheat, but not quite smoking, and then put the beef on.
3. Salt and pepper the beef according to your preferences, and more around continuously with large metal spatulas,
4. Top with cheese, cover with a dome and turn OFF the griddle. The residual heat will melt the cheese.
5. Load up your buns with cheese-covered ribeye, top with any peppers and onions that you want, and chow!

Nutritional Value (Amount per Serving):

Calories: 817; Fat: 70.28; Carb: 6.79; Protein: 39.57

Blackstone Steak Bites

Prep Time: 20 minutes   Cook Time: 15 minutes   Serves: 6

Ingredients:

- 1 1/2 pounds steak, cut into 1" cubes
- 1 tablespoon oil

Sauce
- 1 cup soy sauce
- 1/3 cup vegetable oil
- 1/2 cup pineapple juice
- 2 tablespoons honey
- 1 1/2 teaspoons Sriracha sauce, or a little more if you like it spicier!
- 1 1/2 teaspoons minced garlic

Slurry
- 1 tablespoon cornstarch
- 1/2 cup cold water

Directions:

1. Combine all the sauce ingredients in a 1-gallon ziplock bag and allow the steak to marinate 36-48 hours in the refrigerator.
2. When you are ready to cook, first separate the steak from the marinade, place the steak in a bowl and set it aside.
3. Pour the marinade into a medium saucepan and cook on medium heat until it simmers. Continue cooking for 5 minutes, and then set aside.
4. Combine 1/2 cup cold water with 1 tablespoon of cornstarch and mix until there are no more lumps. Whisk the slurry into the simmering sauce, and continue cooking until it is slightly thickened. Remove from heat and set aside.
5. Preheat your flat-top griddle over medium heat. Lay down a bit of oil and cook the steak for 4-5 minutes, max. Don't overcook it!
6. Remove from the griddle and serve over rice. Drizzle the sauce over the top.

Nutritional Value (Amount per Serving):

Calories: 516; Fat: 33.46; Carb: 21.13; Protein: 34.76

Blackstone Griddle Steak

Prep Time: 5 minutes   Cook Time: 15 minutes   Serves: 1

Ingredients:

- 1 steak
- salt
- pepper

Directions:

Direct Sear Method

1. Preheat your Blackstone to medium-high heat. Season your steak with salt and pepper, and place on the grill.
2. Don't touch it for several minutes so that it will develop a crust.
3. Flip once, and let cook until a crust develops on the other side, and the steak has reached the desired temperature.
4. If your steak is particularly thick, like the one pictured here, you'll want to sear the sides as well. If it is extra thick and also attached to the bone, like a tomahawk or cowboy ribeye, you'll want to reduce the heat to medium-low and cook the steak with a dome or cover over it to ensure even cooking.

Reverse Sear Method

1. Season your meat and place it on a smoker at 180°-200°F. Let the steak reverse sear for about an hour, or until the internal temperature reaches about 120°F.
2. Remove from the pellet grill or smoker, and place onto a preheated flat top

griddle at medium-high to high heat. Let sear for 2-3 minutes per side to develop a crust.

Nutritional Value (Amount per Serving):

Calories: 568; Fat: 27.69; Carb: 4.26; Protein: 76.65

Blackstone Beef Teriyaki

Prep Time: 10 minutes   Cook Time: 10 minutes   Serves: 6

Ingredients:

Steak
- 3 pounds thin sliced steak

Teriyaki Marinade & Sauce
- Homemade Teriyaki Marinade
- 1/2 cup water
- 1 cup pineapple juice
- 1 cup soy sauce
- 3 tablespoons mirin
- 3 tablespoons red miso paste
- 1 tablespoon white vinegar
- 1/2 cup dark brown sugar
- 2 teaspoons minced garlic
- 1/2 teaspoon powdered ginger (or 1/4 teaspoon fresh grated ginger root)
- 2 teaspoons sesame oil
- 3 tablespoons toasted sesame seeds
- 3 green onions, diced (whites and green)
- 2 tablespoons sriracha (optional)
- 1 teaspoon gochujang (optional)

Directions:

1. Add the thin-sliced steak to a large freezer baggie or glass storage container.
2. Mix together all of the marinade ingredients and pour into the container.
3. Marinate the meat for at least 4 hours or up to 12 hours.
4. Preheat your Blackstone over medium-high heat.
5. Remove the meat from the marinade, and place the marinade into a stock pot on the stove. Simmer for 15 minutes over medium-high heat, stirring frequently.
6. Cook the meat on the Blackstone until cooked through. Flip halfway through cooking, and separate the meat if it sticks together.
7. Remove and serve with rice and the extra teriyaki sauce.

Nutritional Value (Amount per Serving):

Calories: 937; Fat: 72.91; Carb: 29.2; Protein: 42.38

Blackstone Pork Chops

Prep Time: 10 minutes   Cook Time: 10 minutes   Serves: 8

Ingredients:

Pork Chop Marinade
- 1 cup water
- 1/4 cup olive oil
- 1/4 cup fresh squeezed lemon juice
- 1 lemon, thinly sliced
- 3 cloves minced garlic
- 2 sprigs fresh thyme
- 1 tablespoon honey
- 1 teaspoon red pepper flakes
- 1/2 teaspoon salt
- 1/2 teaspoon black pepper
- 2 tablespoons apple cider vinegar
- 1 tablespoon chopped parsley

Pork Chops
- 8 pork chops
- 2 teaspoons salt
- 2 teaspoons garlic powder
- 1 teaspoon pepper
- 4 tablespoons oil

Directions:

1. Combine all of the marinade ingredients in a large freezer baggie or a large flat-bottomed storage container. Whisk or mash the baggie together to combine. Add the pork chops and refrigerate the whole thing for 4 hours.
2. Drain the marinade off of the pork chops and pat dry with paper towels.
3. Preheat your Blackstone griddle over medium heat.
4. Mix together the salt, garlic powder, and pepper. Season both sides of the pork chops.
5. Put the oil down on the griddle. You can use less if you prefer. You just want a thin layer of oil on the griddle for the pork to cook in.
6. Brown the chops on both sides. Remove from the griddle when the internal temperature reaches 135°F.
7. Remove from the griddle and tent with foil and let the chops rest for at least 10-15 minutes. The internal temperature will rise by at least 5°F in that time period.
8. Serve hot with your favorite sides. Pictured here you see steamed rice, broccoli, and plenty of Bachan's and sesame seeds on top.

Nutritional Value (Amount per Serving):

Calories: 864; Fat: 55.19; Carb: 7.03; Protein: 81.23

Chapter 8: Snacks & Desserts

Blackstone Griddle French Toast

Prep Time: 10 minutes   Cook Time: 15 minutes   Serves: 6

Ingredients:

- 6 eggs
- 1 teaspoon cinnamon
- 1 teaspoon vanilla
- 1 teaspoon sugar
- 1/4 teaspoon salt
- 12 slices brioche cinnamon swirl bread
- butter
- maple syrup

Directions:

1. Preheat your griddle over low to medium-low heat.
2. Whisk together the eggs, cinnamon, vanilla, sugar, and salt. Make sure it is fully mixed together and you cannot see any egg whites still clinging together.
3. Lay a thin coat of butter onto the griddle surface. Dip the bread, one slice at a time, into the egg wash. Make sure it is totally covered. Place onto the griddle and cook for about 2-3 minutes per side, or until the egg wash is fully set and the surface is getting light golden brown. Flip, and cook for 2-3 minutes on the other side. Repeat until all of the slices are cooked.
4. Serve with extra butter and hot real maple syrup.

Nutritional Value (Amount per Serving):

Calories: 381; Fat: 13.31; Carb: 73.58; Protein: 12.54

Griddle Corn Cakes with Honey Butter

Prep Time: 10 minutes   Cook Time: 20 minutes   Serves: 8

Ingredients:

Corncakes
- 2/3 cup sugar
- 1/4 cup honey
- 1/2 cup melted butter
- 2 large eggs, beaten
- 1/2 teaspoon baking soda
- 1 cup buttermilk
- 1/4 cup 2% or whole milk
- 1/2 teaspoon salt
- 1 cup cornmeal
- 1 cup flour
- Butter for pan

Honey Butter
- 1 stick salted butter, room temp
- 1/4 cup honey

Directions:

1. Mix together all of the corn cake ingredients until most of the lumps are gone. Don't overmix!
2. Heat a skillet over medium heat and melt a little butter on it. Place about 1/4 cup of batter onto the pan, and if necessary smoosh it down a bit into a flat round. Cook until browned, about 2 minutes, and then flip and finish cooking. Repeat with the rest of the batter until all of it has been cooked.
3. Mix honey and 1/2 cup butter together until completely combined. Serve with the hot corn cakes.

Nutritional Value (Amount per Serving):

Calories: 428; Fat: 21.07; Carb: 55.95; Protein: 5.35

Old Fashioned Griddle Cakes

Prep Time: 10 minutes   Cook Time: 10 minutes   Serves: 8

Ingredients:

- 1 cup all-purpose flour
- 1/2 teaspoon baking soda
- 1/4 teaspoon salt
- 1/2 teaspoon baking powder
- 1 cup whole milk, or milk alternative
- 2 tablespoons unsalted butter, melted
- Cooking spray

Directions:

1. Gather the ingredients.
2. In a large bowl, sift flour and add baking soda and salt.
3. In a separate bowl, mix baking powder and milk.
4. Combine dry ingredients with milk and baking powder and stir well with a whisk until the batter is very smooth without clumps.
5. Add melted butter into the batter and mix well for a few seconds.
6. Before putting the griddle on top of the stove, spray it with cooking spray or dampen a paper towel with oil and rub into the griddle surface to grease it. Heat the griddle on medium-high.
7. With the help of a ladle-spoon, pour 1/8 of the batter onto hot griddle to form each griddle cake.
8. When each cake is brown on the bottom and starts to bubble on the top, flip to cook other side.
9. Remove from heat as soon as they are done.
10. Enjoy hot with your favorite toppings!

Nutritional Value (Amount per Serving):

Calories: 103; Fat: 3.02; Carb: 16.14; Protein: 2.66

Fried Mozzarella Balls

Prep Time: 15 minutes   Cook Time: 15 minutes   Serves: 18

Ingredients:

- String Cheese Sticks 3 Sticks
- Flour, All Purpose 1/4 cup
- Breadcrumbs, Italian 3/4 cup
- Egg, Large 1 each
- Milk 2 teaspoons
- Oil for frying

Directions:

1. Gather your ingredients to make the fried mozzarella balls.
2. Set up your dredging station using three bowls. Have one bowl for bread crumbs, place flour in another bowl, and another one with the egg and milk that is beaten together.
3. Use mozzarella pearls or string cheese sticks that have been cut up into pieces. For this recipe, I used small pieces of string cheese sticks.
4. Start with the flour, next dip in the egg mixture, then the breadcrumbs, back into the beaten egg mixture, and then finally the breadcrumbs. Let me repeat this process with a little more explanation. Toss the string cheese piece into the flour and tap off any excess flour. Nest, completely cover the mozzarella pieces with the egg wash. Then, roll the dipped balls into the breadcrumbs to coat completely and evenly. Go back to the egg wash and gently dip the fully breadcrumb coated mozzarella cheese ball with the egg mixture. Finally, coat the mozzarella bites with a beautiful layer of Italian breadcrumbs. Repeat these dredging steps until all the mozzarella cheese balls are coated.
5. Use a baking sheet lined with parchment paper or paper towels to place the fully coated mozzarella balls in a single layer. Freeze the Italian breaded cheese balls for at least 2 hours.
6. To fry the Italian breaded mozzarella balls on a Blackstone Griddle, place a pan on the flat top griddle.
7. Fill the pan halfway or about two inches with your favorite frying oil.
8. Turn the burners of the Blackstone Griddle to high heat.
9. Cover the pan with a large dome lid.
10. Use a digital thermometer to help keep track of the oil temperature. You want the oil to be 375°F.
11. Once the oil reaches 375°F, place the frozen mozzarella balls, one at a time into the hot oil. DO NOT OVERCROWD THE OIL!!
12. With a metal slotted spoon, turn the balls and work in batches if needed.
13. The mozzarella cheesy balls will cook up quickly (2 to 3 minutes), so make sure to keep a close eye on them. When the balls float and turn golden brown, remove the balls from the oil with the metal slotted spoon.
14. Place the cheese balls onto a paper towels lined plate to soak up any excess oil.

15. If you don't have a griddle, you can also use a deep fryer or a small saucepan on the stove with oil to cook your mozzarella balls.
16. Serve with your favorite dipping sauce such as ranch dressing or marinara sauce.

Nutritional Value (Amount per Serving):

Calories: 26; Fat: 0.8; Carb: 2.2; Protein: 2.33

Griddle Flat Bread

Prep Time: 15 minutes   Cook Time: 5 minutes   Serves: 4-5

Ingredients:

- 3 cups all-purpose flour
- 1 cup ice-cold water
- 3 tablespoons shortening, at room temperature
- 2 teaspoons salt
- 2 teaspoons baking powder
- 1 pinch baking soda

Directions:

1. Combine all ingredients and form into a dough.
2. Cover with a clean dishcloth and allow to sit for at least 30 minutes.
3. Cut into 4 or 5 equal pieces. Roll out to a thin 8-inch circle.
4. Prick the surface of the dough with a fork and cook on an oiled hot griddle. Turn with a spatula.
5. Watch these flatbread disks closely because they cook fast.
6. Serve warm.

Nutritional Value (Amount per Serving):

Calories: 429; Fat: 10.53; Carb: 72.71; Protein: 9.69

Ginger Pancakes

Prep Time: 5 minutes   Cook Time: 10 minutes   Serves: 8

Ingredients:

- 2 Cups Baking Mix Gluten-Free or Regular
- 1 Cup Milk
- 2 Eggs
- 1 Teaspoon Vanilla
- 3 Tablespoon Brown Sugar Packed
- 2 Teaspoon Ginger

- 1 Teaspoon Cinnamon
- 1/4 Teaspoon Kosher Salt
- Powdered Sugar Optional
- Maple Syrup Optional

Directions:

1. In a large bowl, whisk together the baking mix and the milk.
2. Whisk in the eggs, vanilla, brown sugar, ginger, cinnamon, and salt.
3. In a greased skillet or griddle, turn it on to medium heat.
4. Then, pour about 1/4 cup of the batter onto the skillet.
5. This will cook until it starts to bubble, then flip over.
6. Continue cooking until all batter has been used, this made 8 pancakes. It will vary though based on size.
7. Sprinkle with powdered sugar as the snow and top with your favorite maple syrup.
8. If you want to add the design in powdered sugar, use a cookie cutter placed on top of the pancake and sprinkle the snow over the pancake, then remove the cookie cutter.

Nutritional Value (Amount per Serving):

Calories: 588; Fat: 20.3; Carb: 95.66; Protein: 8.17

Pumpkin Pancakes

Prep Time: 10 minutes   Cook Time: 15 minutes   Serves: 8

Ingredients:

- 2 Cups All Purpose Flour or Gluten Free All Purpose Flour
- 3 teaspoon Baking Powder or Gluten Free Baking Powder
- 1 teaspoon Salt
- 2 Cups Milk
- 1/2 Cup Sugar
- 2 Eggs
- 1 Tablespoon Vanilla
- 1 Cup Pureed Pumpkin Canned Pumpkin
- 1/2 teaspoon Cinnamon
- 1/2 teaspoon Ground Ginger
- 1 teaspoon Pumpkin Pie Spice

Directions:

1. Combine all ingredients in a mixing bowl in order expect for the toppings.
2. Warm up the griddle or skillet on the stove to about 350°F or medium-high heat. Coat with nonstick cooking spray.
3. Spoon out the batter into about sand dollar size and let it cook on one side

until the batter begins to bubble, then flip over and cook until done. This typically just takes 2-3 minutes; however, I went about 5 minutes or more to be sure the inside is fully cooked. The pumpkin sometimes takes a bit longer to cook the middle.

4. It should release fairly easily from the griddle and you can be sure that the bottom is browned.
5. Continue until all pancake batter is used.
6. Top them with a dash of Pumpkin Pie Spice or Cinnamon along with warm syrup or caramel!

Nutritional Value (Amount per Serving):

Calories: 156; Fat: 6.73; Carb: 17.61; Protein: 6.29

Gluten-Free Pancakes with Homemade Bisquick

Prep Time: 10 minutes   Cook Time: 9 minutes   Serves: 8

Ingredients:

- 2 Cups Homemade Bisquick
- 1 1/3 Cup Milk
- 2 Whole Eggs

Directions:

1. Preheat a griddle or skillet to 350°F.
2. Add the dry ingredients to a medium sized bowl, then mix in the wet ingredients until your batter is formed. Add additional milk if needed if it is too thick.
3. Once your batter is formed and the griddle is coated with non-stick spray if needed, add about 1/3 cup of pancake mix
4. Cook for 4-5 minutes or until golden brown, flip and cook an additional 2-3 minutes.
5. Serve with warm maple syrup and blueberries or toppings of choice.

Nutritional Value (Amount per Serving):

Calories: 126; Fat: 4.2; Carb: 15.55; Protein: 6.57

Blackstone Loaded Potato Chips

Prep Time: 10 minutes   Cook Time: 10 minutes   Serves: 4

Ingredients:

- 2 russet potatoes
- vegetable oil (I keep mine in a squirt bottle)
- kosher salt, pepper

- 1 1/2 cups shredded cheese of choice
- 5 strips cooked and crumbled bacon
- Optional: ranch, sour cream, chives

Directions:

1. Preheat the Blackstone to medium high heat. While it heats up, slice the potatoes into 1/4 inch slices.
2. Add some oil to the griddle and spread evenly with a spatula. Put the potatoes on the griddle for 5 to 6 minutes per side. Season both sides with kosher salt and pepper.
3. Turn the grill off, top each potato chip with cheese and bacon crumbles. Once melted remove from the griddle.
4. Serve with ranch or sour cream and chives if desired.

Nutritional Value (Amount per Serving):

Calories: 370; Fat: 18.37; Carb: 35.35; Protein: 16.83

Gluten-Free Fluffy Blueberry Pancakes

Prep Time: 40 minutes   Cook Time: 10 minutes   Serves: 8

Ingredients:

- 2 Cups All Purpose Flour or Gluten Free All Purpose Flour
- 3 Teaspoon Baking Powder or Gluten Free Baking Powder
- 1 Teaspoon Salt
- 2 Cups Milk
- 1/2 Cup Sugar
- 2 Eggs
- 1 Tablespoon Vanilla
- 1-2 Cups Blueberries

Directions:

1. Combine all ingredients in a bowl mixing well use a whisk or spatula to combine. Add in the blueberries last, fold these in carefully.
2. Let batter sit for about 30 minutes for fluffier pancakes.
3. While the batter is sitting about 10 minutes before you are ready to cook begin to heat the griddle or skillet to medium heat and spray with non stick cooking spray.
4. Spoon out the batter into about sand dollar size and let it cook on one side until the batter begins to bubble, then flip over and cook until done.
5. This typically just takes 2-3 minutes. It should release fairly easily from the griddle and you can be sure that the bottom is browned.
6. Continue until all pancake batter is used.
7. Serve with syrup and butter or your favorite toppings!

Nutritional Value (Amount per Serving):

Calories: 186; Fat: 6.77; Carb: 25.36; Protein: 6.24

Blackstone Griddle Grilled Nachos

Prep Time: 5 minutes   Cook Time: 5 minutes   Serves: 10

Ingredients:

- Olive Oil 1 tablespoon
- Ground Beef 1 pound
- Taco Seasoning 2 tablespoons
- Tortilla Strips 12 ounces
- Water 2 tablespoons
- Shredded Cheese 2 cups
- Tomato, Diced 1/2 cup
- Peppers, Bell 1/4 cup
- Sour Cream 2 tablespoons
- Lettuce, Shredded 1/2 cup

Directions:

1. Preheat the Blackstone Flat Top Griddle to medium heat.
2. Prepare your diced tomatoes, peppers and lettuce.
3. As the Blackstone Griddle is heating up, apply the olive oil and spread with a griddle spatula.
4. When the griddle is hot and nearly smoking, add ground hamburger to the griddle. Cook the ground burger, breaking it up as you go, until it is in small pieces and no longer pink inside.
5. Make sure to separate as much of the ground beef grease from the cooked burger as possible before adding the taco seasoning. Push the excess grease into the grease trap.
6. Top the cooked burger with the taco seasoning. Add a squirt of water to help combine the ground beef and taco seasoning,
7. When the meat mixture is cooked, place tortilla chips on a prepared baking sheet pan or serving dish lined with parchment paper.
8. Top the tortilla chips with the hot beef mixture, and the shredded cheese.
9. If desired place the whole sheet pan with the chips, burger and cheese onto the the hot Blackstone Griddle and cover with a large dome lid for about 2 - 3 minutes to melt the cheese.
10. Choose your desired toppings. Sprinkle the toppings like chopped bell peppers, diced tomatoes, shredded lettuce, and of course, a dollop of sour cream.
11. Serve hot and make sure to have a variety of side, if possible, that your guests will like.

Nutritional Value (Amount per Serving):

Calories: 384; Fat: 17.97; Carb: 30.67; Protein: 23.3

Easy Blueberry Cobbler

Prep Time: 5 minutes   Cook Time: 30 minutes   Serves: 1

Ingredients:

- Blueberries (Fresh or Frozen) 1 cup
- Sugar, Granulated 1 tablespoon
- Flour, All Purpose 1 teaspoon
- Cake Batter, Yellow (mixed per directions) 1/3 cup

Directions:

1. Preheat the Blackstone Griddle to a low setting.
2. Gather your ingredients to make your old-fashioned blueberry cobbler.
3. Clean, rinse, and drain the fresh blueberries.
4. Using the 8-ounce ramekins, place the blueberries into it. Make sure to only fill about 1/2 way with blueberries.
5. Add the sugar and flour on top of the blueberries. Stir to combine all ingredients.
6. Top the blueberry mixture with the cake batter. Do not fill past the inner rim. Otherwise, the cake batter will run all over the place.
7. Place a piece of parchment paper down on the hot griddle flat top. This helps to prevent the griddle from smoking and giving your cobbler a funky smoke flavor.
8. On the preheated Blackstone griddle, place the ramekins and cover with a dome lid. This creates the oven effect to bake the blueberry cobbler.
9. Bake for 30 minutes and test for doneness by inserting a toothpick into the top cake batter only. If the toothpick comes out clean, then the blueberry cobbler with cake mix is done. If the wooden toothpick comes out wet with batter, then cook longer.
10. When the toothpick comes out clean, remove from the flat top griddle.
11. Eat the blueberry cobbler piping hot with a dollop of ice cream or let cool for later.

Nutritional Value (Amount per Serving):

Calories: 603; Fat: 2.22; Carb: 139.47; Protein: 7.99

APPENDIX RECIPE INDEX

Made in the USA
Middletown, DE
29 August 2024

59989324R00062